CAPITALISM
A GHOST STORY

CAPITALISM
A GHOST STORY

Arundhati Roy

Haymarket Books
Chicago, Illinois

First published by Haymarket Books in 2014

Haymarket Books
P.O. Box 180165, Chicago, IL 60618
773-583-7884
info@haymarketbooks.org
www.haymarketbooks.org

ISBN: 978-160846-385-5

Trade distribution:
In the US, through Consortium Book Sales and Distribution, www.cbsd.com
In Canada, through Publishers Group Canada, www.pgcbooks.ca

Special discounts are available for bulk purchases by organizations and institutions. Please contact Haymarket Books for more information at 773-583-7884 or info@haymarketbooks.org.

This book was published with the generous support of Lannan Foundation and the Wallace Action Fund.

Cover design by Abby Weintraub.

Printed in Canada by union labor.

Library of Congress CIP data is available.

5 7 9 10 8 6 4

CONTENTS

Your blood asks, how were the wealthy
and the law interwoven? With what
sulfurous iron fabric? How did the
poor keep falling into the tribunals?

How did the land become so bitter
for poor children, harshly
nourished on stone and grief?
So it was, and so I leave it written.
Their lives wrote it on my brow.

Pablo Neruda
"The Judges"[1]

PREFACE

THE PRESIDENT TOOK THE SALUTE

The Minister says that for India's sake, people should leave their villages and move to the cities. He's a Harvard man. He wants speed. And numbers. Five hundred million migrants he thinks, will make a good business model.

Not everybody likes the idea of their cities filling up with the poor. A judge in Bombay called slum dwellers pickpockets of urban land. Another said, while ordering the bulldozing of unauthorized colonies, that people who couldn't afford to live in cities shouldn't live in them.

When those who had been evicted went back to where they came from, they found their villages had disappeared under great dams and dusty quarries. Their homes were occupied by hunger—and policemen. The forests were filling up with armed guerrillas. They found that the wars from the edge of India, in Kashmir, Nagaland, Manipur, had migrated to its heart. People returned to live on city streets and pavements, in hovels on dusty construction sites, wondering which corner of this huge country was meant for them.

The Minister said that migrants to cities were mostly criminals and "carried a kind of behavior which is unacceptable to modern cities."[1] The middle class admired him for his forthrightness, for having the courage to call a spade a spade. The Minister said he would set up more police stations, recruit more policemen, and put more police vehicles on the road to improve law and order.

In the drive to beautify Delhi for the Commonwealth Games, laws were passed that made the poor vanish, like laundry stains. Street vendors disappeared, rickshaw pullers lost their licenses, small shops and businesses were shut down. Beggars were rounded up, tried by mobile magistrates in mobile courts, and dropped outside the city limits. The slums that remained were screened off, with vinyl billboards that said DELHIciously Yours.

New kinds of policemen patrolled the streets, better armed, better dressed, and trained not to scratch their privates in public, no matter how grave the provocation. There were cameras everywhere, recording everything.

◆

Two young criminals carrying a kind of behavior that was unacceptable to modern cities escaped the police dragnet and approached a woman sitting between her sunglasses and the leather seats of her shiny car at a traffic crossing. Shamelessly they demanded money. The woman was rich and kind. The criminals' heads were no higher than her car window. Their names were Rukmini and Kamli. Or maybe Mehrunissa and Shahbano. (Who cares.) The woman gave them money and some motherly advice. Ten rupees to Kamli (or Shahbano). "Share it," she told them, and sped away when the lights changed.

Rukmini and Kamli (or Mehrunissa and Shahbano) tore into each other like gladiators, like lifers in a prison yard. Each sleek car that flashed past them, and almost crushed them, carried the reflection of their battle, their fight to the finish, on its shining door.

Eventually both girls disappeared without a trace, like thousands of children do in Delhi.

The Games were a success.

◆

Two months later, on the sixty-second anniversary of India's Republic Day, the armed forces showcased their new weapons at the Republic Day parade: a missile launcher system, Russian multi-barrel rocket launchers, combat aircraft, light helicopters, and underwater weapons for the navy. The new T-90 battle tank was called Bhishma. (The older one was Arjun.) Varunastra was the name of the latest heavyweight torpedo, and Mareech was a decoy system to seduce incoming torpedoes. (Hanuman and Vajra are the names painted on the armored vehicles that patrol Kashmir's frozen streets.) The names from the Bhagavad Gita, the Ramayana, and the Mahabharata were a coincidence. Dare Devils from the Army's Corps of Signals rode motorcycles in a rocket formation; then they formed a cluster of flying birds and finally a human pyramid.

The army band played the national anthem. The President took the salute.

Three Sukhoi fighter jets made a Trishul in the sky. Shiva's Trishul. Is India a Hindu republic? Only accidentally.

The thrilled crowd turned its face up to the weak winter sun and applauded the aerobatics. High in the sky, the winking silver sides of the jets carried the reflection of Rukmini and Kamli's (or Mehrunissa and Shahbano's) fight to the death.

SECTION ONE

CHAPTER 1

CAPITALISM: A GHOST STORY

Is it a house or a home? A temple to the new India or a warehouse for its ghosts? Ever since Antilla arrived on Altamount Road in Mumbai, exuding mystery and quiet menace, things have not been the same. "Here we are," the friend who took me there said. "Pay your respects to our new Ruler."

Antilla belongs to India's richest man, Mukesh Ambani. I'd read about this most expensive dwelling ever built, the twenty-seven floors, three helipads, nine lifts, hanging gardens, ballrooms, weather rooms, gymnasiums, six floors of parking, and six hundred servants. Nothing had prepared me for the vertical lawn—a soaring, twenty-seven-story-high wall of grass attached to a vast metal grid. The grass was dry in patches; bits had fallen off in neat rectangles. Clearly, Trickledown hadn't worked.

But Gush-Up certainly has. That's why in a nation of 1.2 billion, India's one hundred richest people own assets equivalent to one-fourth of the GDP.[1]

The word on the street (and in the *New York Times*) is, or at least was, that after all that effort and gardening, the Ambanis don't live in Antilla.[2] No one knows for sure. People still whisper about ghosts and bad luck, Vastu and feng shui. Maybe it's all Karl Marx's fault. (All that cussing.) Capitalism, he said, "has conjured up such gigantic means of production and of exchange, that it is like the sorcerer who is no longer able to control the powers of the netherworld whom he has called up by his spells."[3]

In India the 300 million of us who belong to the new, post–International Monetary Fund (IMF) "reforms" middle class—the market—live side by side with spirits of the netherworld, the poltergeists of dead rivers, dry wells, bald mountains, and denuded forests; the ghosts of 250,000 debt-ridden farmers who have killed themselves, and of the 800 million who have been impoverished and dispossessed to make way for us.[4] And who survive on less than twenty Indian rupees a day.[5]

Mukesh Ambani is personally worth $20 billion.[6] He holds a majority controlling share in Reliance Industries Limited (RIL), a company with a market capitalization of $47 billion and global business interests that include petrochemicals, oil, natural gas, polyester fiber, Special Economic Zones, fresh food retail, high schools, life sciences research, and stem cell storage services. RIL recently bought 95 percent shares in Infotel, a TV consortium that controls twenty-seven TV news and entertainment channels, including CNN-IBN, IBN Live, CNBC, IBN Lokmat, and ETV in almost every regional language.[7] Infotel owns the only nationwide license for 4G broadband, a high-speed information pipeline which, if the technology works, could be the future of information exchange.[8] Mr. Ambani also owns a cricket team.

RIL is one of a handful of corporations that run India. Some of the others are the Tatas, Jindals, Vedanta, Mittals, Infosys, Essar, and the other Reliance, Reliance Anil Dhirubhai Ambani Group (ADAG), owned by Mukesh's brother Anil. Their race for growth has spilled across Europe, Central Asia, Africa, and Latin America. Their nets are cast wide; they are visible and invisible, over ground as well as underground. The Tatas, for example, run more than one hundred companies in eighty countries. They are one of India's oldest and largest private-sector power companies. They own mines, gas fields, steel plants, telephone, and cable TV and broadband networks, and run whole townships. They manufacture cars and trucks and own the Taj Hotel chain, Jaguar, Land Rover, Daewoo, Tetley Tea, a publishing company, a chain of bookstores, a major brand of iodized salt, and the cosmetics giant Lakme. Their advertising tagline could easily be You Can't Live Without Us.

According to the rules of the Gush-Up Gospel, the more you have, the more you can have.

The era of the Privatization of Everything has made the Indian economy one of the fastest growing in the world. However, as with any good old-fashioned colony, one of its main exports is its minerals. India's new megacorporations, Tatas, Jindals, Essar, Reliance, Sterlite, are those that have managed to muscle their way to the head of the spigot that is spewing money extracted from deep inside the earth.[9] It's a dream come true for businessmen—to be able to sell what they don't have to buy.

The other major source of corporate wealth comes from their land banks. All over the world, weak, corrupt local governments have helped Wall Street brokers, agribusiness corporations, and Chinese billionaires to amass huge tracts of land. (Of course this entails commandeering water too.) In India the land of millions of people is being acquired and handed over to private corporations for "public interest"—for Special Economic Zones (SEZs), infrastructure projects, dams, highways, car manufacture, chemical hubs, and Formula One racing.[10] (The sanctity of private property never applies to the poor.) As always, local people are promised that their displacement from their land and the expropriation of everything they ever had is actually part of employment generation. But by now we know that the connection between GDP growth and jobs is a myth. After twenty years of "growth," 60 percent of India's workforce is self-employed, and 90 percent of India's labor force works in the unorganized sector.[11]

Post-Independence, right up to the 1980s, people's movements, ranging from the Naxalites to Jayaprakash Narayan's Sampoorna Kranti, were fighting for land reforms, for the redistribution of land from feudal landlords to landless peasants. Today any talk of redistribution of land or wealth would be considered not just undemocratic but lunatic. Even the most militant movements have been reduced to a fight to hold on to what little land people still have. The millions of landless people, the majority of them Dalits and Adivasis, driven from their villages, living in slums and shanty colonies in small towns and megacities, do not figure even in the radical discourse.

As Gush-Up concentrates wealth onto the tip of a shining pin on which our billionaires pirouette, tidal waves of money crash through the institutions of democracy—the courts, the parliament—as well as the media, seriously compromising their ability to function in the ways they are meant to. The noisier the carnival around elections, the less sure we are that democracy really exists.

Each new corruption scandal that surfaces in India makes the last one look tame. In the summer of 2011 the 2G spectrum scandal broke. We learned that corporations had siphoned away $40 billion of public money by installing a friendly soul as the minister of communications and information who grossly underpriced the licenses for 2G telecom spectrums and illegally auctioned them to his buddies. The taped telephone conversations leaked to the press showed how a network of industrialists and their front companies, ministers, senior journalists, and a TV anchor were involved in facilitating this daylight robbery. The tapes were just an MRI that confirmed a diagnosis that people had made long ago.

The privatization and illegal sale of telecom spectrum does not involve war, displacement, and ecological devastation. The privatization of India's mountains, rivers, and forests does. Perhaps because it does not have the uncomplicated clarity of a straightforward, out-and-out accounting scandal, or perhaps because it is all being done in the name of India's "progress," it does not have the same resonance with the middle classes.

In 2005 the state governments of Chhattisgarh, Orissa, and Jharkhand signed hundreds of memorandums of understanding (MOUs) with a number of private corporations, turning over trillions of dollars of bauxite, iron ore, and other minerals for a pittance, defying even the warped logic of the Free Market. (Royalties to the government ranged between 0.5 percent and 7 percent.)[12]

Only days after the Chhattisgarh government signed an MOU for the construction of an integrated steel plant in Bastar with Tata Steel, the Salwa Judum, a vigilante militia, was inaugurated. The government said it was a spontaneous uprising of local people who were fed up with "repression" by Maoist guerillas in the forest. It turned out to be a ground-clearing operation, funded and armed by the government and subsidized by mining corporations. In the other states similar militias were created, with other names. The prime minister announced the Maoists were the "Single Largest Security Challenge in India." It was a declaration of war.[13]

On January 2, 2006, in Kalinganagar, in the neighboring state of Orissa, perhaps to signal the seriousness of the government's intention, ten platoons of police arrived at the site of another Tata Steel plant and opened fire on villagers who had gathered there to protest what they felt was inadequate compensation for their land. Thirteen people, including one policeman, were killed and thirty-seven injured.[14] Six years have gone by, and though the villages remain under siege by armed policemen, the protest has not died.

Meanwhile in Chhattisgarh, the Salwa Judum burned, raped, and murdered its way through hundreds of forest villages, evacuating six hundred villages and forcing 50,000 people to come out into police camps and 350,000 people to flee.[15] The chief minister announced that those who did not come out of the forests would be considered "Maoist terrorists." In this way, in parts of modern India plowing fields and sowing seed came to be defined as terrorist activity. Eventually the Salwa Judum's atrocities succeeded only in strengthening the resistance and swelling the ranks of the Maoist guerilla army. In 2009 the government announced what it called Operation Green Hunt. Two hundred thousand paramilitary troops were deployed across Chhattisgarh, Orissa, Jharkhand, and West Bengal.[16]

After three years of "low-intensity conflict" that has not managed to "flush" the rebels out of the forest, the central government has declared that it will deploy the Indian army and air force.[17] In India we don't call this war. We call it "Creating a Good Investment Climate." Thousands of soldiers have already moved in. A brigade headquarters and airbases are being readied. One of the biggest armies in the world is now preparing its Terms of Engagement to "defend" itself against the poorest, hungriest, most malnourished people in the world. We only await the declaration of the Armed Forces Special Powers Act (AFSPA), which will give the army legal impunity and the right to kill "on suspicion." Going by the tens of thousands of unmarked graves and anonymous cremation pyres in Kashmir, Manipur, and Nagaland, we might judge it to be a very suspicious army indeed.[18]

While the preparations for deployment are being made, the jungles of Central India continue to remain under siege, with villagers frightened to come out or to go to the market for food or medicine. Hundreds of people have been jailed, charged with being Maoists under draconian, undemocratic laws. Prisons are crowded with Adivasi people, many of whom have no idea what their crime is. Recently, Soni Sori, an Adivasi schoolteacher from

Bastar, was arrested and tortured in police custody. Stones were pushed up her vagina to get her to "confess" that she was a Maoist courier. The stones were removed from her body at a hospital in Calcutta, where, after a public outcry, she was sent for a medical checkup. At a recent Supreme Court hearing, activists presented the judges with the stones in a plastic bag. The only outcome of their efforts has been that Soni Sori remains in jail, while Ankit Garg, the superintendent of police who conducted the interrogation, was conferred the President's Police Medal for Gallantry on Republic Day.[19]

We hear about the ecological and social reengineering of Central India only because of the mass insurrection and the war. The government gives out no information. The MOUs are all secret. Some sections of the media have done what they could to bring public attention to what is happening in Central India. However, most of the Indian mass media is made vulnerable by the fact that the major share of their revenues come from corporate advertisements. If that is not bad enough, now the line between the media and big business has begun to blur dangerously. As we have seen, RIL virtually owns twenty-seven TV channels. But the reverse is also true. Some media houses now have direct business and corporate interests. For example, one of the major daily newspapers in the region, *Dainik Bhaskar*—and it is only one example—has 17.5 million readers in four languages, including English and Hindi, across thirteen states. It also owns sixty-nine companies with interests in mining, power generation, real estate, and textiles. A recent writ petition filed in the Chhattisgarh High Court accuses DB Power Ltd (one of the group's companies) of using "deliberate, illegal and manipulative measures" through company-owned newspapers to influence the outcome of a public hearing over an open cast coalmine.[20] Whether or not it has attempted to influence the outcome is not germane. The point is that media houses are in a position to do so. They have the power to do so. The laws of the land allow them to be in a position that lends itself to a serious conflict of interest.

There are other parts of the country from which no news comes. In the sparsely populated but militarized northeastern state of Arunachal Pradesh, 168 big dams are being constructed, most of them privately owned.[21] High dams that will submerge whole districts are being constructed in Manipur and Kashmir, both highly militarized states where people can be killed merely for protesting power cuts. (That happened a few weeks ago in Kashmir.)[22] How can they stop a dam?

The most delusional dam of all is the Kalpasar in Gujarat. It is being planned as a 34-km-long dam across the Gulf of Khambat with a ten-lane highway and a railway line running on top of it. The idea is to keep out the seawater and create a sweet-water reservoir of Gujarat's rivers. (Never mind that these rivers have already been dammed to a trickle and poisoned with chemical effluent.) The Kalpasar dam, which would raise the sea level and alter the ecology of hundreds of kilometers of coastline, was the cause of serious concerns amongst scientists in a 2007 report.[23] It has made a sudden comeback in order to supply water to the Dholera Special Investment Region (SIR) in one of the most water-stressed zones not just in India but in the world. SIR is another name for a SEZ, a self-governed corporate dystopia of industrial parks, townships, and megacities. The Dholera SIR is going to be connected to Gujarat's other cities by a network of ten-lane highways. Where will the money for all this come from?

In January 2011 in the Mahatma (Gandhi) Mandir, Gujarat's Chief Minister Narendra Modi presided over a meeting of ten thousand international businessmen from one hundred countries. According to media reports, they pledged to invest $450 billion in Gujarat. The meeting was deliberately scheduled to take place on the tenth anniversary of the massacre of two thousand Muslims in February 2002. Modi stands accused of not just condoning but actively abetting the killing. People who watched their loved ones being raped, eviscerated, and burned alive, the tens of thousand who were driven from their homes, still wait for a gesture toward justice. But Modi has traded in his saffron scarf and vermillion forehead for a sharp business suit and hopes that a $450 billion investment will work as blood money and square the books.[24] Perhaps it will. Big Business is backing him enthusiastically. The algebra of infinite justice works in mysterious ways.

The Dholera SIR is only one of the smaller Matryoshka dolls, one of the inner ones in the dystopia that is being planned. It will be connected to the Delhi Mumbai Industrial Corridor (DMIC), a 1,500-km-long and 300-km-wide corridor with nine megaindustrial zones, a high-speed freight line, three seaports, six airports, a six-lane intersection-free expressway, and a 4,000-mw power plant. The DMIC is a collaborative venture between the governments of India and Japan, and their respective corporate partners, and has been proposed by the McKinsey Global Institute.

The DMIC website says that approximately 180 million people will be "affected" by the project.[25] Exactly how it doesn't say. It envisages the building of several new cities and estimates that the population in the region will grow from the current 231 million to 314 million by 2019. That's in seven years' time. When was the last time a state, despot, or dictator carried out a population transfer of millions of people? Can it possibly be a peaceful process?

The Indian army might need to go on a recruitment drive so that it's not taken unawares when it is ordered to deploy all over India. In preparation for its role in Central India, it publicly released its updated doctrine of military psychological operations, which outlines "a planned process of conveying a message to a select target audience, to promote particular themes that result in desired attitudes and behaviour, which affect the achievement of political and military objectives of the country." This process of "perception management," it said, would be conducted by "using media available to the Services."[26]

The army is experienced enough to know that coercive force alone cannot carry out or manage social engineering on the scale that is envisaged by India's planners. War against the poor is one thing. But for the rest of us—the middle class, white-collar workers, intellectuals, "opinion-makers"—it has to be "perception management." And for this we must turn our attention to the exquisite art of Corporate Philanthropy.

Of late, the main mining conglomerates have embraced the arts—film, art installations, and the rush of literary festivals that have replaced the 1990s obsession with beauty contests. Vedanta, currently mining the heart out of the homelands of the ancient Dongria Kond tribe for bauxite, is sponsoring a "Creating Happiness" film competition for young film students whom it has commissioned to make films on sustainable development. Vedanta's tagline is "Mining Happiness." The Jindal Group brings out a contemporary art magazine and supports some of India's major artists (who naturally work with stainless steel). Essar was the principal sponsor of the Tehelka Newsweek Think Fest that promised "high-octane debates" by the foremost thinkers from around the world, which included major writers, activists, and even the architect Frank Gehry.[27] (All this in Goa, where activists and journalists were uncovering massive illegal mining scandals, and Essar's part in the war unfolding in Bastar was emerging.)[28] Tata Steel and Rio Tinto (which has a sordid track record of its own) were among the chief sponsors of the Jaipur Literary Festival (Latin name: Darshan Singh Construction Jaipur Literary Festival), which is advertised by the cognoscenti as "The Greatest Literary Show on Earth." Counselage, the Tatas "strategic brand manager," sponsored the festival's press tent. Many of the world's best and brightest writers gathered in Jaipur to discuss love, literature, politics, and Sufi poetry. Some tried to defend Salman Rushdie's right to free speech by reading from his proscribed book, *The Satanic Verses*. In every TV frame and newspaper photograph the logo of Tata Steel (and its tagline, Values Stronger than Steel) loomed behind them, a benign, benevolent host. The enemies of free speech were the supposedly murderous Muslim mobs, who, the festival organizers told us, could have even harmed the schoolchildren gathered there. (We are witness to how helpless the Indian government and the police can be when it comes to Muslims.) Yes, the hardline Darul-uloom Deobandi Islamic seminary did protest Rushdie's being invited to the festival. Yes, some Islamists did gather at the festival venue to protest, and yes, outrageously, the state government did nothing to protect the venue. That's because the whole episode had as much to do with democracy, vote banks, and the Uttar Pradesh (UP) elections as it did with Islamist fundamentalism. But the battle for Free Speech against Islamist Fundamentalism made it to the world's newspapers. It is important that it did. But there were hardly any reports about the festival sponsors' role in the war in the forests, the bodies piling up, the prisons filling up. Or about the Unlawful Activities Prevention Act and the Chhattisgarh Special Public Security Act, which make even *thinking* an antigovernment thought a cognizable offense. Or about the mandatory public hearing for the Tata Steel plant in Lohandiguda, which local people complained actually took place hundreds of miles away in Jagdalpur, in the collector's office compound, with a hired audience of fifty people, under armed guard.[29] Where was Free Speech then? No one mentioned Kalinganagar. No one mentioned that journalists, academics, and filmmakers working on subjects unpopular with the Indian government—like the surreptitious part it played in the genocide of Tamils in the war in Sri Lanka, or the recently discovered unmarked graves in Kashmir—were being denied visas or deported straight from the airport.[30]

But which of us sinners was going to cast the first stone? Not me, who lives off royalties from corporate publishing houses. We all watch Tata Sky, we surf the Net with Tata Photon, we ride in Tata taxis, we stay in Tata Hotels, sip our Tata tea in Tata bone china, and stir it with teaspoons made of Tata Steel. We buy Tata books in Tata bookshops. *Hum Tata ka namak khatey hain.* We're under siege.

If the sledgehammer of moral purity is to be the criteria for stone throwing, then the only people who qualify are those who have been silenced already. Those who live outside the system; the outlaws in the forests, or those whose protests are never covered by the press, or the well-behaved Dispossessed, who go from tribunal to tribunal, bearing witness, giving testimony.

But the Litfest gave us our Aha! Moment. Oprah came.[31] She said she *loved* India, that she would come *again* and *again*. It made us proud.

This is only the burlesque end of the Exquisite Art.

Though the Tatas have been involved with corporate philanthropy for almost a hundred years now, endowing scholarships and running some excellent educational institutes and hospitals, Indian corporations have only recently been invited into the Star Chamber, the *Camera stellata*, the brightly lit world of global corporate government, deadly for its adversaries but otherwise so artful that you barely know it's there.

What follows in this essay might appear to some to be a

somewhat harsh critique. On the other hand, in the tradition of honoring one's adversaries, it could be read as an acknowledgment of the vision, flexibility, sophistication, and unwavering determination of those who have dedicated their lives to keeping the world safe for capitalism.

Their enthralling history, which has faded from contemporary memory, began in the United States in the early twentieth century when, kitted out legally in the form of endowed foundations, corporate philanthropy began to replace missionary activity as Capitalism's (and Imperialism's) road-opening and systems maintenance patrol.[32]

Among the first foundations to be set up in the United States were the Carnegie Corporation, endowed in 1911 by profits from Carnegie Steel Company, and the Rockefeller Foundation, endowed in 1914 by J. D. Rockefeller, founder of Standard Oil Company. The Tatas and Ambanis of their time.

Some of the institutions financed, given seed money, or supported by the Rockefeller Foundation are the United Nations, the CIA, the Council on Foreign Relations (CFR), New York's most fabulous Museum of Modern Art, and, of course, the Rockefeller Center in New York (where Diego Riviera's mural had to be blasted off the wall because it mischievously depicted reprobate capitalists and a valiant Lenin; Free Speech had taken the day off).

Rockefeller was America's first billionaire and the world's richest man. He was an abolitionist, a supporter of Abraham Lincoln, and a teetotaler. He believed his money was given to him by God, which must have been nice for him.[33]

Here are a few verses from one of Pablo Neruda's early poems called "Standard Oil Company":

> Their obese emperors from New York
> are suave smiling assassins
> who buy silk, nylon, cigars
> petty tyrants and dictators.
> They buy countries, people, seas, police, county councils,
> distant regions where the poor hoard their corn
> like misers their gold:
> Standard Oil awakens them,
> clothes them in uniforms, designates
> which brother is the enemy.
> The Paraguayan fights its war,
> and the Bolivian wastes away
> in the jungle with its machine gun.
> A President assassinated for a drop of petroleum,
> a million-acre mortgage,
> a swift execution on a morning mortal with light, petrified,
> a new prison camp for subversives,
> in Patagonia, a betrayal, scattered shots
> beneath a petroliferous moon,
> a subtle change of ministers
> in the capital, a whisper
> like an oil tide,
> and zap, you'll see
> how Standard Oil's letters shine above the clouds,
> above the seas, in your home,
> illuminating their dominions.[34]

When corporate-endowed foundations first made their appearance in the United States, there was a fierce debate about their provenance, legality, and lack of accountability. People suggested that if companies had so much surplus money, they should raise the wages of their workers. (People made these outrageous suggestions in those days, even in America.) The idea of these foundations, so ordinary now, was in fact a leap of the business imagination. Non-tax-paying legal entities with massive resources and an almost unlimited brief—wholly unaccountable, wholly nontransparent—what better way to parlay economic wealth into political, social, and cultural capital, to turn money into power? What better way for usurers to use a minuscule percentage of their profits to run the world? How else would Bill Gates, who admittedly knows a thing or two about computers, find himself designing education, health, and agriculture policies, not just for the US government but for governments all over the world?[35]

Over the years, as people witnessed some of the genuinely good work the foundations did (running public libraries, eradicating diseases)—the direct connection between corporations and the foundations they endowed began to blur. Eventually, it faded altogether. Now even those who consider themselves left wing are not shy to accept their largesse.

By the 1920s US capitalism had begun to look outward for raw materials and overseas markets. Foundations began to formulate the idea of global corporate governance. In 1924 the Rockefeller and Carnegie Foundations jointly created what is today the most powerful foreign policy pressure group in the world—the Council on Foreign Relations (CFR), which later came to be funded by the Ford Foundation as well. By 1947 the newly created CIA was supported by and working closely with the CFR. Over the years the CFR's membership has included twenty-two US secretaries of state. There were five CFR members in the 1943 steering committee that planned the United Nations, and an $8.5 million grant from J. D. Rockefeller bought the land on which the United Nations' New York headquarters stands.[36]

All eleven of the World Bank's presidents since 1946—men who have presented themselves as missionaries to the poor—have been members of the CFR. (The exception was George Woods. And he was a trustee of the Rockefeller Foundation and vice president of Chase Manhattan Bank.)[37]

At Bretton Woods, the World Bank and IMF decided that the US dollar should be the reserve currency of the world, and that in order to enhance the penetration of global capital it would be necessary to universalize and standardize business practices in an open marketplace.[38] It is toward that end that they spend a large amount of money promoting Good Governance (as long as they control the strings), the concept of the Rule of Law (provided they have a say in making the laws), and hundreds of anticorruption programs (to streamline the system they have put in place). Two of the most opaque, unaccountable organizations in the world go about demanding transparency and accountability from the governments of poorer countries.

Given that the World Bank has more or less directed the economic policies of the Third World, coercing and cracking open the market of country after country for global finance, you could say that corporate philanthropy has turned out to be the most visionary business of all time.

Corporate-endowed foundations administer, trade, and channel their power and place their chessmen on the chessboard through a system of elite clubs and think tanks, whose members overlap and move in and out through the revolving doors. Contrary to the various conspiracy theories in circulation, particularly among left-wing groups, there is nothing secret, satanic, or Freemason-like about this arrangement. It is not very different from the way corporations use shell companies and offshore accounts to transfer and administer their money—except that the currency is power, not money.

The transnational equivalent of the CFR is the Trilateral Commission, set up in 1973 by David Rockefeller, the former US national security adviser Zbignew Brzezinski (founder-member of the Afghan mujahidin, forefathers of the Taliban), the Chase Manhattan Bank, and some other private eminences. Its purpose was to create an enduring bond of friendship and cooperation between the elites of North America, Europe, and Japan. It has now become a pentalateral commission, because it includes members from China and India (Tarun Das of the CII; N. R. Narayana Murthy, ex-CEO of Infosys; Jamsheyd N. Godrej, managing director of Godrej; Jamshed J. Irani, director of Tata Sons; and Gautam Thapar, CEO of Avantha Group).[39]

The Aspen Institute is an international club of local elites, businessmen, bureaucrats, and politicians, with franchises in several countries. Tarun Das is the president of the Aspen Institute, India. Gautam Thapar is chairman. Several senior officers of the

McKinsey Global Institute (proposer of the Delhi Mumbai Industrial Corridor) are members of the CFR, the Trilateral Commission, and the Aspen Institute.[40]

The Ford Foundation (liberal foil to the more conservative Rockefeller Foundation, though the two work together constantly) was set up in 1936. Though it is often underplayed, the Ford Foundation has a very clear, well-defined ideology and works extremely closely with the US State Department. Its project of deepening democracy and "good governance" is very much part of the Bretton Woods scheme of standardizing business practice and promoting efficiency in the free market. After the Second World War, when communists replaced fascists as the US Government's Enemy Number One, new kinds of institutions were needed to deal with the Cold War. Ford funded RAND (Research and Development Corporation), a military think tank that began with weapons research for the US defense services. In 1952, to thwart "the persistent Communist effort to penetrate and disrupt free nations," it established the Fund for the Republic, which then morphed into the Center for the Study of Democratic Institutions, whose brief was to wage the Cold War intelligently, without McCarthyite excesses.[41] It is through this lens that we need to view the work that the Ford Foundation is doing with the millions of dollars it has invested in India—its funding of artists, filmmakers, and activists, its generous endowment of university courses and scholarships.

The Ford Foundation's declared "goals for the future of mankind" include interventions in grassroots political movements locally and internationally. In the United States it provided millions in grants and loans to support the credit union movement that was pioneered by the department store owner Edward Filene in 1919. Filene believed in creating a mass consumption society of consumer goods by giving workers affordable access to credit—a radical idea at the time. Actually, only half of a radical idea, because the other half of what Filene believed in was a more equitable distribution of national income. Capitalists seized on the first half of Filene's suggestion and, by disbursing "affordable" loans of tens of millions of dollars to working people, turned the US working class into people who are permanently in debt, running to catch up with their lifestyles.[42]

Many years later, this idea has trickled down to the impoverished countryside of Bangladesh when Mohammed Yunus and the Grameen Bank brought microcredit to starving peasants with disastrous consequences. The poor of the subcontinent have always lived in debt, in the merciless grip of the local village usurer—the Baniya. But microfinance has corporatized that too. Microfinance companies in India are responsible for hundreds of suicides—two hundred people in Andhra Pradesh in 2010 alone. A national daily recently published a suicide note by an eighteen-year-old girl who was forced to hand over her last 150 rupees, her school fees, to bullying employees of the microfinance company. The note read, "Work hard and earn money. Do not take loans."[43]

There's a lot of money in poverty, and a few Nobel Prizes too.

By the 1950s the Rockefeller and Ford Foundations, funding several NGOs and international educational institutions, began to work as quasi-extensions of the US government, which was at the time toppling democratically elected governments in Latin America, Iran, and Indonesia. (That was also around the time it made its entry into India, then non-aligned but clearly tilting toward the Soviet Union.) The Ford Foundation established a US-style economics course at the Indonesian University. Elite Indonesian students, trained in counterinsurgency by US army officers, played a crucial part in the 1965 CIA-backed coup in Indonesia that brought General Suharto to power. He repaid his mentors by slaughtering hundreds of thousands of communist rebels.[44]

Twenty years later, young Chilean students, who came to be known as the Chicago Boys, were taken to the United States to be trained in neoliberal economics by Milton Friedman at the University of Chicago (endowed by J. D. Rockefeller), in preparation for the 1973 CIA-backed coup that killed Salvador Allende and brought in General Pinochet and a reign of death squads, disappearances, and terror that lasted for seventeen years.[45] Allende's crime was being a democratically elected socialist and nationalizing Chile's mines.

In 1957 the Rockefeller Foundation established the Ramon Magsaysay Prize for community leaders in Asia. It was named after Ramon Magsaysay, president of the Philippines, a crucial ally in the US campaign against communism in Southeast Asia. In 2000 the Ford Foundation established the Ramon Magsaysay Emergent Leadership Award. The Magsaysay Award is considered a prestigious award among artists, activists, and community workers in India. M. S. Subulakshmi and Satyajit Ray won it, and so did Jaiprakash Narain and one of India's finest journalists, P. Sainath. But they did more for the Magsaysay award than it did for them. In general, it has become a gentle arbiter of what kind of activism is "acceptable" and what is not.[46]

Interestingly, Anna Hazare's anticorruption movement last summer was spearheaded by three Magsaysay Award winners—Anna Hazare, Arvind Kejriwal, and Kiran Bedi. One of Arvind Kejriwal's many NGOs is generously funded by the Ford Foundation. Kiran Bedi's NGO is funded by Coca-Cola and Lehman Brothers.

Though Anna Hazare calls himself a Gandhian, the law he called for—the Jan Lokpal Bill—was un-Gandhian, elitist, and dangerous. An around-the-clock corporate media campaign proclaimed him to be the voice of "the people." Unlike the Occupy Wall Street movement in the United States, the Hazare movement didn't breathe a word against privatization, corporate power, or economic "reforms." On the contrary, its principal media backers successfully turned the spotlight away from massive corporate corruption scandals (which had exposed high-profile journalists too) and used the public mauling of politicians to call for the further withdrawal of discretionary powers from government, for more reforms, more privatization. The World Bank issued a 2007 assessment from Washington saying the movement would "dovetail" with its "good governance" strategy.[47] (In 2008 Anna Hazare received a World Bank Award for Outstanding Public Service.)[48]

Like all good Imperialists, the Philanthropoids set themselves the task of creating and training an international cadre that believed that Capitalism, and by extension the hegemony of the

United States, was in their own self-interest. And who would therefore help to administer the Global Corporate Government in the ways native elites had always served colonialism. So began the foundations' foray into education and the arts, which would become their third sphere of influence, after foreign and domestic economic policy. They spent (and continue to spend) millions of dollars on academic institutions and pedagogy.

Joan Roelofs, in her wonderful book *Foundations and Public Policy: The Mask of Pluralism*, describes how foundations remodeled the old ideas of how to teach political science and fashioned the disciplines of "international" and "area" studies. This provided the US Intelligence and Security Services a pool of expertise in foreign languages and culture to recruit from. The CIA and US State Department continue to work with students and professors in US universities, raising serious questions about the ethics of scholarship.[49]

The gathering of information to control people is fundamental to any ruling power. As resistance to land acquisition and the new economic policies spreads across India, in the shadow of outright war in Central India, as a containment technique, India's government has embarked on a massive biometrics program, perhaps one of the most ambitious and expensive information gathering projects in the world—the Unique Identification Number (UID). People don't have clean drinking water, or toilets, or food, or money, but they will have election cards *and* UID numbers. Is it a coincidence that the UID project run by Nandan Nilekani, former CEO of Infosys, ostensibly meant to "deliver services to the poor," will inject massive amounts of money into a slightly beleaguered IT industry?[50] To digitize a country with such a large population of the illegitimate and "illegible"—people who are for the most part slum dwellers, hawkers, Adivasis without land records—will criminalize them, turning them from illegitimate to illegal. The idea is to pull off a digital version of the Enclosure of the Commons and put huge powers into the hands of an increasingly hardening police state. Nilekani's technocratic obsession with gathering data is consistent with Bill Gates's obsession with digital databases, numerical targets, and "scorecards of progress" as though it were a lack of information that is the cause of world hunger, and not colonialism, debt, and skewed profit-oriented corporate policy.[51]

Corporate-endowed foundations are the biggest funders of the social sciences and the arts, endowing courses and student scholar ships in development studies, community studies, cultural studies, behavioral sciences, and human rights.[52] As US universities opened their doors to international students, hundreds of thousands of students, children of the Third World elite, poured in. Those who could not afford the fees were given scholarships. Today in countries like India and Pakistan there is scarcely a family among the upper middle classes that does not have a child who has studied in the United States. From their ranks have come good scholars and academics but also the prime ministers, finance ministers, economists, corporate lawyers, bankers, and bureaucrats who helped to open up the economies of their countries to global corporations.

Scholars of the foundations-friendly version of economics and political science were rewarded with fellowships, research funds, grants, endowments, and jobs. Those with foundation-unfriendly views found themselves unfunded, marginalized, and ghettoized, their courses discontinued. Gradually, one particular imagination—a brittle, superficial pretense of tolerance and multiculturalism (that morphs into racism, rabid nationalism, ethnic chauvinism, or war-mongering Islamophobia at a moment's notice) under the roof of a single overarching, very unplural economic ideology—began to dominate the discourse. It did so to such an extent that it ceased to be perceived as an ideology at all. It became the default position, the natural way to be. It infiltrated normality, colonized ordinariness, and challenging it began to seem as absurd or as esoteric as challenging reality itself. From here it was a quick, easy step to "There Is No Alternative."

It is only now, thanks to the Occupy movement, that another language has appeared on US streets and campuses. To see students with banners that say "Class War" or "We don't mind you being rich, but we mind you buying our government" is, given the odds, almost a revolution in itself.

One century after it began, corporate philanthropy is as much part of our lives as Coca-Cola. There are now millions of nonprofit organizations, many of them connected through a byzantine financial maze to the larger foundations. Between them, this "independent" sector has assets worth nearly $450 billion. The largest of them is the Gates Foundation with $21 billion, followed by the Lilly Endowment ($16 billion) and the Ford Foundation ($15 billion).[53]

As the IMF enforced structural adjustment and arm-twisted governments into cutting back on public spending on health, education, child care, development, the NGOs moved in.[54] The Privatization of Everything has also meant the NGO-ization of Everything. As jobs and livelihoods disappeared, NGOs have become an important source of employment, even for those who see them for what they are. And they are certainly not all bad. Of the millions of NGOs, some do remarkable, radical work, and it would be a travesty to tar all NGOs with the same brush. However, the corporate or foundation-endowed NGOs are global finance's way of buying into resistance movements, literally as shareholders buy shares in companies, and then try to control them from within. They sit like nodes on the central nervous system, the pathways along which global finance flows. They work like transmitters, receivers, shock absorbers, alert to every impulse, careful never to annoy the governments of their host countries. (The Ford Foundation requires the organizations it funds to sign a pledge to this effect.) Inadvertently (and sometimes advertently) they serve as listening posts, their reports and workshops and other missionary activity feeding data into an increasingly aggressive system of surveillance of increasingly hardening states. The more troubled an area, the greater the numbers of NGOs in it.

Mischievously, when India's government or sections of its corporate press want to run a smear campaign against a genuine people's movement, like the Narmada Bachao Andolan, or the protest against the Koodankulam nuclear reactor, they accuse these movements of being NGOs receiving "foreign funding." They know very well that the mandate of most NGOs, in particular the well-funded ones, is to further the project of corporate globalization, not thwart it.

Armed with their billions, these NGOs have waded into the world, turning potential revolutionaries into salaried activists, funding artists, intellectuals, and filmmakers, gently luring them away from radical confrontation, ushering them in the direction of multiculturalism, gender equity, community development—the discourse couched in the language of identity politics and human rights.

The transformation of the idea of justice into the industry of human rights has been a conceptual coup in which NGOs and foundations have played a crucial part. The narrow focus of human rights enables an atrocity-based analysis in which the larger picture can be blocked out and both parties in a conflict—say for example the Maoists and the Indian government, or the Israeli army and Hamas—can both be admonished as Human Rights Violators. The land grab by mining corporations and the history of the annexation of Palestinian land by the state of Israel then become footnotes with very little bearing on the discourse. This is not to suggest that human rights don't matter. They do, but they are not a good enough prism through which to view or remotely understand the great injustices in the world we live in.

Another conceptual coup has to do with foundations' involvement with the feminist movement. Why do most "official" feminists and women's organizations in India keep a safe distance between themselves and organizations like say the ninety-thousand-member Krantikari Adivasi Mahila Sanghatan (Revolutionary Adivasi Women's Association) that is fighting patriarchy in its own communities and displacement by mining corporations in the Dandakaranya forest? Why is it that the dispossession and eviction of millions of women from land that they owned and worked is not seen as a feminist problem?

The hiving off of the liberal feminist movement from grassroots anti-imperialist and anticapitalist peoples' movements did not begin with the evil designs of foundations. It began with those movements' inability to adapt and accommodate the rapid radicalization of women that took place in the 1960s and '70s. The foundations showed genius in recognizing and moving in to support and fund women's growing impatience with the violence and patriarchy in their traditional societies as well as among even the supposedly progressive leaders of left movements. In a country like India, the schism also ran along the rural-urban divide. Most radical, anticapitalist movements were located in the countryside, where patriarchy continued to rule the lives of women. Urban women activists who joined these movements (like the Naxalite movement) had been influenced and inspired by the Western feminist movement, and their own journeys toward liberation were often at odds with what their male leaders considered to be their duty: To fit in with "the masses." Many women activists were not willing to wait any longer for the "revolution" in order to end the daily oppression and discrimination in their lives, including from their own comrades. They wanted gender equality to be an absolute, urgent, and nonnegotiable part of the revolutionary process and not just a postrevolution promise. Intelligent, angry, and disillusioned women began to move away and look for other means of support and sustenance. As a result, by the late 1980s, around the time when the Indian markets were opened up, the liberal feminist movement in India had become inordinately NGO-ized. Many of these NGOs have done seminal work on queer rights, domestic violence, AIDS, and the rights of sex workers. But significantly, the liberal feminist movement has not been at the forefront of challenging the New Economic Policies, even though women have been the greatest sufferers. By manipulating the disbursement of the funds, the foundations have largely succeeded in circumscribing the range of what "political" activity should be. The funding briefs of NGOs now prescribe what counts as women's "issues" and what doesn't.

The NGO-ization of the women's movement has also made Western liberal feminism (by virtue of its being the most funded brand) the standard-bearer of what constitutes feminism. The battles, as usual, have been played out on women's bodies, extruding Botox at one end and burkas at the other. (And then there are those who suffer the double whammy, Botox *and* the burka.) When, as happened recently in France, an attempt is made to coerce women out of the burka rather than creating a situation in which a woman can choose what she wishes to do, it's not about liberating her but about unclothing her. It becomes an act of humiliation and cultural imperialism. Coercing a woman out of her burka is as bad as coercing her into one. It's not about the burka. It's about the coercion. Viewing gender in this way, shorn of social, political, and economic context, makes it an issue of identity, a battle of props and costumes. It's what allowed the US government to use Western feminist liberal groups as moral cover when it invaded Afghanistan in 2001. Afghan women were (and are) in terrible trouble under the Taliban. But dropping daisy cutters on them was not going to solve the problem.

In the NGO universe, which has evolved a strange anodyne language of its own, everything has become a "subject," a separate, professionalized, special-interest issue. Community development, leadership development, human rights, health, education, reproductive rights, AIDS, orphans with AIDS—have all been hermetically sealed into their own silos, each with its own elaborate and precise funding brief. Funding has fragmented solidarity in ways that repression never could.

Poverty, too, like feminism, is often framed as an identity problem. As though the poor had not been created by injustice but are a lost tribe who who just happen to *exist*, and can be rescued in the short term by a system of grievance redressal (administered by NGOs on an individual, person-to-person basis), and whose long-term resurrection will come from Good Governance. Under the regime of Global Corporate Capitalism, it goes without saying.

Indian poverty, after a brief period in the wilderness while India "shone," has made a comeback as an exotic identity in the arts, led from the front by films like *Slumdog Millionaire*. These stories about the poor, their amazing spirit and resilience, have no villains—except the small ones who provide narrative tension and local color. The authors of these works are the contemporary world's equivalent of the early anthropologists, lauded and honored for working "on the ground," for their brave journeys into the unknown. You rarely see the rich being examined in these ways.

Having worked out how to manage governments, political parties, elections, courts, the media, and liberal opinion, the neoliberal establishment faced one more challenge: how to deal with growing unrest, the threat of "peoples' power." How do you domesticate it? How do you turn protesters into pets? How do you vacuum up people's fury and redirect it into blind alleys?

Here too, foundations and their allied organizations have a long and illustrious history. A revealing example is their role in defusing and deradicalizing the Black civil rights movement in the United States in the 1960s and the successful transformation of Black Power into Black Capitalism.[55]

The Rockefeller Foundation, in keeping with J. D. Rockefeller's ideals, had worked closely with Martin Luther King Sr. (father of Martin Luther King Jr.). But his influence waned with the rise of the more militant organizations—the Student Non-Violent Coordinating Committee (SNCC) and the Black Panthers. The Ford and Rockefeller Foundations moved in. In 1970 they donated $15 million to "moderate" Black organizations, giving people, grants, fellowships, scholarships, job-training programs for dropouts, and seed money for Black-owned businesses.[56] Repression, infighting, and the honey trap of funding led to the gradual atrophying of the radical Black organizations.

Martin Luther King Jr. made the forbidden connections between Capitalism, Imperialism, Racism, and the Vietnam War. As a result, after he was assassinated even his memory became toxic, a threat to public order. Foundations and corporations worked hard to remodel his legacy to fit a market-friendly format. The Martin

Luther King Jr. Center for Nonviolent Social Change, with an operational grant of $2 million, was set up by, among others, the Ford Motor Company, General Motors, Mobil, Western Electric, Proctor and Gamble, US Steel, and Monsanto. The center maintains the King Library and Archives of the Civil Rights Movement. Among the many programs the King Center runs have been projects that "work closely with the United States Department of Defense, the Armed Forces Chaplains Board and others."[57] It cosponsored the Martin Luther King Jr. Lecture Series called "The Free Enterprise System: An Agent for Nonviolent Social Change."[58]

Amen.

A similar coup was carried out in the antiapartheid struggle in South Africa. In 1978 the Rockefeller Foundation organized a Study Commission on US Policy toward Southern Africa. The report warned of the growing influence of the Soviet Union on the African National Congress (ANC) and said that US strategic and corporate interests (that is, access to South Africa's minerals) would be best served if there were genuine sharing of political power by all races.

The foundations began to support the ANC. The ANC soon turned on the more radical organizations like Steve Biko's Black Consciousness movement and more or less eliminated it. When Nelson Mandela took over as South Africa's first Black president, he was canonized as a living saint, not just because he is a freedom fighter who spent twenty-seven years in prison but also because he deferred completely to the Washington Consensus. Socialism disappeared from the ANC's agenda. South Africa's great "peaceful transition," so praised and lauded, meant no land reforms, no demands for reparation, no nationalization of South Africa's mines. Instead there was privatization and structural adjustment. Mandela gave South Africa's highest civilian award—the Order of Good Hope—to his old friend and supporter General Suharto, the killer of communists in Indonesia. Today in South Africa, a clutch of Mercedes-driving former radicals and trade unionists rule the country. But that is more than enough to perpetuate the myth of Black liberation.

The rise of Black Power in the United States was an inspirational moment for the rise of a radical, progressive Dalit movement in India, with organizations like the Dalit Panthers mirroring the militant politics of the Black Panthers. But Dalit Power too, in not exactly the same but similar ways, has been fractured and defused and, with plenty of help from right-wing Hindu organizations and the Ford Foundation, is well on its way to transforming into Dalit Capitalism.

"Dalit Inc ready to show business can beat caste," the *Indian Express* reported in December last year. It went on to quote a mentor of the Dalit Indian Chamber of Commerce and Industry (DICCI): "Getting the prime minister for a Dalit gathering is not difficult in our society. But for Dalit entrepreneurs, taking a photograph with Tata and Godrej over lunch and tea is an aspiration—and proof that they have arrived," he said.[59] Given the situation in modern India, it would be casteist and reactionary to say that Dalit entrepreneurs oughtn't to have a place at the high table. But if this were to be the aspiration, the ideological framework of Dalit politics, it would be a great pity. And unlikely to help the one million Dalits who still earn a living off manual scavenging—carrying human shit on their heads.

Young Dalit scholars who accept grants from the Ford Foundation cannot be too harshly judged. Who else is offering them an opportunity to climb out of the cesspit of the Indian caste system? The shame as well as a large part of the blame for this turn of events also goes to India's communist movement, whose leaders continue to be predominantly upper caste. For years it has tried to force-fit the idea of caste into Marxist class analysis. It has failed miserably, in theory as well as practice. The rift between the Dalit community and the Left began with a falling out between the visionary Dalit leader Bhimrao Ambedkar and S. A. Dange, trade unionist and founding member of the Communist Party of India. Dr. Ambedkar's disillusionment with the Communist Party began with the textile workers' strike in Mumbai in 1928, when he realized that despite all the rhetoric about working-class solidarity, the party did not find it objectionable that the "untouchables" were kept out of the weaving department (and qualified only for the lower-paid spinning department) because the work involved the use of saliva on the threads, which other castes considered "polluting."

Ambedkar realized that in a society where the Hindu scriptures institutionalize untouchability and inequality, the battle for "untouchables," for social and civic rights, was too urgent to wait for the promised communist revolution. The rift between the Ambedkarites and the Left has come at a great cost to both. It has meant that a great majority of the Dalit population, the backbone of the Indian working class, has pinned its hopes for deliverance and dignity on constitutionalism, capitalism, and political parties like the Bahujan Samaj Party (BSP), which practices an important, but in the long run stagnant, brand of identity politics.

In the United States, as we have seen, corporate-endowed foundations spawned the culture of NGOs. In India, targeted corporate philanthropy began in earnest in the 1990s, the era of the New Economic Policies. Membership in the Star Chamber doesn't come cheap. The Tata Group donated $50 million to that needy institution the Harvard Business School, and another $50 million to Cornell University. Nandan Nilekani of Infosys and his wife Rohini donated $5 million as a startup endowment for the India Initiative at Yale. The Harvard Humanities Center is now the Mahindra Humanities Center, after it received its largest-ever donation of $10 million from Anand Mahindra of the Mahindra Group.

At home, the Jindal Group, with a major stake in mining, metals, and power, runs the Jindal Global Law School and will soon open the Jindal School of Government and Public Policy. (The Ford Foundation runs a law school in the Congo.) The New India Foundation, funded by Nandan Nilekani, financed by profits from Infosys, gives prizes and fellowships to social scientists. The Sitaram Jindal Foundation, endowed by the chairman and managing director of Jindal Aluminum Ltd, has announced five annual cash prizes of ten million rupees each, to be given to those working in rural development, poverty alleviation, education and moral uplift, environment, and peace and social harmony. The

Observer Research Foundation (ORF), currently endowed by Mukesh Ambani, is cast in the mold of the Rockefeller Foundation. It has retired intelligence agents, strategic analysts, politicians (who pretend to rail against each other in Parliament), journalists, and policy makers as its research "fellows" and advisers.

ORF's objectives seem straightforward enough: "to help develop a consensus in favor of economic reforms." And to shape and influence public opinion, creating "viable, alternative policy options in areas as divergent as employment generation in backward districts and real-time strategies to counter Nuclear, Biological and Chemical threats."[60]

I was initially puzzled by the preoccupation with "nuclear, biological and chemical threats" in ORF's stated objectives. But less so when, in the long list of its "institutional partners," I found the names of Raytheon and Lockheed Martin, two of the world's leading weapons manufacturers. In 2007 Raytheon announced it was turning its attention to India.[61] Could it be that at least part of India's $32 billion annual defense budget will be spent on weapons, guided missiles, aircraft, warships, and surveillance equipment made by Raytheon and Lockheed Martin?

Do we need weapons to fight wars? Or do we need wars to create a market for weapons? After all, the economies of Europe, the United States, and Israel depend hugely on their weapons industry. It's the one thing they haven't outsourced to China.

In the new cold war between the United States and China, India is being groomed to play the role Pakistan played as a US ally in the Cold War with Russia. (And look what happened to

Pakistan.) Many of those columnists and "strategic analysts" who are playing up the hostilities between India and China, you'll see, can be traced back directly or indirectly to the Indo-American think tanks and foundations. Being a "strategic partner" of the United States does not mean that the heads of state make friendly phone calls to each other every now and then. It means collaboration (interference) at every level. It means hosting US Special Forces on Indian soil (a Pentagon commander recently confirmed this to the BBC). It means sharing Intelligence, altering agriculture and energy policies, opening up the health and education sectors to global investment. It means opening up retail. It means an unequal partnership in which India is being held close in a bear hug and waltzed around the floor by a partner who will incinerate her the moment she refuses to dance.

In the list of ORF's "institutional partners" you will also find the RAND Corporation, the Ford Foundation, the World Bank, the Brookings Institution (whose stated mission is to "provide innovative and practical recommendations that advance three broad goals: strengthen American democracy; foster the economic and social welfare, security and opportunity of all Americans; and secure a more open, safe, prosperous, and cooperative international system"). You will also find the Rosa Luxemburg Foundation of Germany. (Poor Rosa, who died for the cause of communism, to find her name on a list such as this one!)

Though capitalism is meant to be based on competition, those at the top of the food chain have also shown themselves to be capable of inclusiveness and solidarity. The great Western Capitalists have done business with fascists, socialists, despots, and military dictators. They can adapt and constantly innovate. They are capable of quick thinking and immense tactical cunning.

But despite having successfully powered through economic reforms, despite having waged wars and militarily occupied countries in order to put in place free market "democracies," Capitalism is going through a crisis whose gravity has not revealed itself completely yet. Marx said, "What the bourgeoisie therefore produces, above all, are its own grave-diggers. Its fall and the victory of the proletariat are equally inevitable."[62]

The proletariat, as Marx saw it, has been under continuous assault. Factories have shut down, jobs have disappeared, trade unions have been disbanded. Those making up the proletariat have, over the years, been pitted against each other in every possible way. In India it has been Hindu against Muslim, Hindu against Christian, Dalit against Adivasi, caste against caste, region against region. And yet all over the world they are fighting back. In China there are countless strikes and uprisings. In India the poorest people in the world have fought back to stop some of the richest corporations in their tracks.

Capitalism is in crisis. Trickledown failed. Now Gush-Up is in trouble too. The international financial meltdown is closing in. India's growth rate has plummeted to 6.9 percent. Foreign investment is pulling out. Major international corporations are sitting on huge piles of money, not sure where to invest it, not sure how the financial crisis will play out. This is a major, structural crack in the juggernaut of global capital.

Capitalism's real "gravediggers" may end up being its own delusional cardinals, who have turned ideology into faith. Despite their strategic brilliance, they seem to have trouble grasping a simple fact: Capitalism is destroying the planet. The two old tricks that dug it out of past crises—War and Shopping—simply will not work.

I stood outside Antilla for a long time watching the sun go down. I imagined that the tower was as deep as it was high. That it had a twenty-seven-story-long tap root, snaking around below the ground, hungrily sucking sustenance out of the earth, turning it into smoke and gold.

Why did the Ambanis choose to call their building Antilla? Antilla is the name of a set of mythical islands whose story dates back to an eighth-century Iberian legend. When the Muslims conquered Hispania, six Christian Visigothic bishops and their parishioners boarded ships and fled. After days, or maybe weeks, at sea, they arrived at the isles of Antilla, where they decided to settle and raise a new civilization. They burned their boats to permanently sever their links to their barbarian-dominated homeland.

By calling their tower Antilla, do the Ambanis hope to sever their links to the poverty and squalor of their homeland and raise a new civilization? Is this the final act of the most successful secessionist movement in India: the secession of the middle and upper classes into outer space?

As night fell over Mumbai, guards in crisp linen shirts with crackling walkie-talkies appeared outside the forbidding gates of

Antilla. The lights blazed on, to scare away the ghosts perhaps. The neighbors complain that Antilla's bright lights have stolen the night.

Perhaps it's time for us to take back the night.

CHAPTER 2

I'D RATHER NOT BE ANNA

While his means may be Gandhian, his demands are certainly not.

If what we're watching on TV is indeed a revolution, then it has to be one of the more embarrassing and unintelligible ones of recent times. For now, whatever questions you may have about the Jan Lokpal Bill, here are the answers you're likely to get—tick the box: (a) "Vande Mataram" (I bow to thee, Mother); (b) "Bharat Mata ki Jai" (victory for Mother India); (c) India is Anna, Anna is India; (d) "Jai Hind" (hail India).

For completely different reasons, and in completely different ways, you could say that the Maoists and the Jan Lokpal Bill have one thing in common—they both seek the overthrow of the Indian state. One working from the bottom up, by means of an armed struggle, waged by a largely Adivasi army, made up of the poorest of the poor. The other from the top down, by means of a bloodless Gandhian coup, led by a freshly minted saint and an army of largely urban and certainly better-off people. (In this one, the government collaborates by doing everything it possibly can to overthrow itself.)

In April 2011, a few days into Anna Hazare's first "fast unto death," searching for some way of distracting attention from the massive corruption scams which had battered its credibility, the government invited Team Anna, the brand name chosen by this "civil society" group, to be part of a joint drafting committee for a new anticorruption law.[1] A few months down the line it abandoned that effort and tabled its own bill in Parliament, a bill so flawed that it was impossible to take seriously.

Then, on August 16, the morning of his second "fast unto death," before he had begun his fast or committed any legal offense, Anna Hazare was arrested and jailed. The struggle for the implementation of the Jan Lokpal Bill now coalesced into a struggle for the right to protest, the struggle for democracy itself. Within hours of this "Second Freedom Struggle," Anna was released. Cannily, he refused to leave prison but remained in the Tihar jail as an honored guest, where he began a fast, demanding the right to fast in a public place. For three days, while crowds and television vans gathered outside, members of Team Anna whizzed in and out of the high-security prison, carrying out his video messages to be broadcast on national TV on all channels. (Which other person would be granted this luxury?) Meanwhile 250 employees of the Municipal Commission of Delhi, fifteen trucks, and six earth movers worked around the clock to ready the slushy Ramlila grounds for the grand weekend spectacle. Now, waited upon hand and foot, watched over by chanting crowds and crane-mounted cameras, attended to by India's most expensive doctors, the third phase of Anna's fast to the death has begun. "From Kashmir to Kanyakumari, India is One," the TV anchors tell us.[2]

While his means may be Gandhian, Anna Hazare's demands are certainly not. Contrary to Gandhiji's ideas about the decentralization of power, the Jan Lokpal Bill is a draconian anticorruption law, in which a panel of carefully chosen people will administer a giant bureaucracy, with thousands of employees, with the power to police everybody from the prime minister, the judiciary, members of Parliament, and all of the bureaucracy, down to the lowest government official. The Lokpal will have the powers of investigation, surveillance, and prosecution. Except for the fact that it won't have its own prisons, it will function as an independent administration, meant to counter the bloated, unaccountable, corrupt one that we already have. Two oligarchies, instead of just one.

Whether it works or not depends on how we view corruption. Is corruption just a matter of legality, of financial irregularity and bribery, or is it the currency of a social transaction in an egregiously unequal society, in which power continues to be concentrated in the hands of a smaller and smaller minority? Imagine, for example, a city of shopping malls, on whose streets hawking has been banned. A hawker pays the local beat cop and the man from the municipality a small bribe to break the law and sell her wares to those who cannot afford the prices in the malls. Is that such a terrible thing? In the future will she have to pay the Lokpal representative too? Does the solution to the problems faced by ordinary people lie in addressing the structural inequality or in creating yet another power structure that people will have to defer to?

Meanwhile the props and the choreography, the aggressive nationalism and flag-waving of Anna's Revolution are all borrowed from the antireservation protests, the World Cup victory parade, and the celebration of the nuclear tests. They signal to us that if we do not support The Fast, we are not "true Indians." The twenty-four-hour channels have decided that there is no other news in the country worth reporting.

"The Fast" of course doesn't mean Irom Sharmila's fast that has lasted for more than ten years (she's being force-fed now) against the Armed Forces Special Powers Act (AFSPA), which allows soldiers in Manipur to kill merely on suspicion. It does not mean the relay hunger fast that is going on by ten thousand villagers in Koodankulam protesting against the nuclear power plant. "The People" does not mean the Manipuris who support Irom Sharmila's fast. Nor does it mean the thousands who are facing down armed policemen and mining mafias in Jagatsinghpur, or Kalinganagar, or Niyamgiri, or Bastar, or Jaitapur. Nor do we mean the victims of the Bhopal gas leak, or the people displaced by dams in the Narmada Valley. Nor do we mean the farmers in the New Okhla Industrial Development Area (NOIDA), or Pune or Haryana or elsewhere in the country, resisting the takeover of the land.

"The People" means only the audience that has gathered to watch the spectacle of a seventy-four-year-old man threatening to starve himself to death if his Jan Lokpal Bill is not tabled and passed by Parliament. "The People" are the tens of thousands who have been miraculously multiplied into millions by our TV channels, as Christ multiplied the fishes and loaves to feed the hungry. "A billion voices have spoken," we're told. "India is Anna."

Who is he really, this new saint, this Voice of the People? Oddly enough, we've heard him say nothing about things of urgent concern. Nothing about the farmer's suicides in his neighborhood, or about Operation Green Hunt farther away. Nothing about Singur, Nandigram, Lalgarh, nothing about Posco, about farmers' agitations or the blight of SEZs. He doesn't seem to have a view about the government's plans to deploy the Indian army in the forests of Central India.

He does, however, support Raj Thackeray's Marathi Manoos xenophobia and has praised the "development model" of Gujarat's chief minister, who oversaw the 2002 pogrom against Muslims. (Anna withdrew that statement after a public outcry, but presumably not his admiration.)[3]

Despite the din, sober journalists have gone about doing what journalists do. We now have the backstory about Anna's old relationship with the right-wing Rashtriya Swayamsevak Sangh (RSS).[4] We have heard from Mukul Sharma, who has studied Anna's village community in Ralegan Siddhi, where there have been no Gram Panchayat or cooperative society elections in the last twenty-five years. We know about Anna's attitude to "harijans": "It was Mahatma Gandhi's vision that every village should have one chamar, one sunar, one kumhar and so on. They should all do their work according to their role and occupation, and in this way, a village will be self-dependent. This is what we are practicing in Ralegan Siddhi."[5]

Is it surprising that members of Team Anna have also been associated with Youth for Equality, the antireservation (pro-"merit") movement? The campaign is being handled by people who run a clutch of generously funded NGOs whose donors include Coca-Cola and the Lehman Brothers. Kabir, run by Arvind Kejriwal and Manish Sisodia, key figures in Team Anna, has received $400,000 from the Ford Foundation in the last three years.[6] Among contributors to the India Against Corruption campaign there are Indian companies and foundations that own aluminum plants, build ports and Special Economic Zones (SEZs), run real estate businesses, and are closely connected to politicians who oversee financial empires that run into thousands of crores of rupees. Some of them are currently being investigated for corruption and other crimes. Why are they all so enthusiastic?

Remember, the campaign for the Jan Lokpal Bill gathered steam around the same time as embarrassing revelations by Wikileaks and a series of scams, including the 2G spectrum scam, broke, in which major corporations, senior journalists, and government ministers and politicians from the Congress as well as the BJP seem to have colluded in various ways as hundreds of thousands of crores of rupees were being siphoned off from the public exchequer. For the first time in years, journalist-lobbyists were disgraced, and it seemed as if some major captains of Corporate India could actually end up in prison. Perfect timing for a people's anticorruption agitation. Or was it?

At a time when the state is withdrawing from its traditional duties and corporations and NGOs are taking over government functions (water supply, electricity, transport, telecommunications, mining, health, education); at a time when the corporate-owned media with its terrifying power and reach is trying to control the public imagination, one would think that these institutions—the corporations, the media, and the NGOs—would be included in the jurisdiction of a Lokpal bill. Instead, the proposed bill leaves them out completely.

Now, by shouting louder than everyone else, by pushing a campaign that is hammering away at the theme of evil politicians and government corruption, they have very cleverly let themselves off the hook. Worse, by demonizing only the government they have built themselves a pulpit from which to call for the further withdrawal of the state from the public sphere and for a second round of reforms—more privatization, more access to public infrastructure and India's natural resources. It may not be long before Corporate Corruption is made legal and renamed a Lobbying Fee.

Will the 830 million people living on twenty rupees a day really benefit from the strengthening of a set of policies that is impoverishing them and driving this country to civil war?

This awful crisis has been forged out of the utter failure of India's representative democracy, in which the legislatures are made up of criminals and millionaire politicians who have ceased to represent its people. In which not a single democratic institution is accessible to ordinary people. Do not be fooled by the flag waving. We're watching India being carved up in war for suzerainty that is as deadly as any battle being waged by the warlords of Afghanistan, only with much, much more at stake.

CHAPTER 3

DEAD MEN TALKING

On September 23, 2011, at about three o'clock in the morning, within hours of his arrival at the Delhi airport, the US radio-journalist David Barsamian was deported.[1] This dangerous man, who produces independent, free-to-air programs for public radio, has been visiting India for forty years, doing dangerous things like learning Urdu and playing the sitar. He has published book-length interviews with Edward Said, Noam Chomsky, Howard Zinn, Eqbal Ahmad, and Tariq Ali. (He even makes an appearance as a young, bell-bottom-wearing interviewer in Peter Wintonik's documentary film based on Chomsky and Edward S. Herman's *Manufacturing Consent.*) On his more recent trips to India he has done a series of radio interviews with activists, academics, filmmakers, journalists, and writers (including me). Barsamian's work has taken him to Turkey, Iran, Syria, Lebanon, and Pakistan. He has never been deported from any of these countries.

So why does the world's largest democracy fear this lone sitar-playing, Urdu-speaking, left-leaning radio producer? Here is how Barsamian himself explains it: "It's all about Kashmir. I've done work on Jharkand, Chhattisgarh, West Bengal, Narmada dams, farmer suicides, the Gujarat pogrom, and the Binayak Sen case. But it's Kashmir that is at the heart of the Indian state's concerns. The official narrative must not be contested."

News reports about his deportation quoted official "sources" as saying that Barsamian had "violated his visa norms during his visit in 2009–10 by indulging in professional work while holding a tourist visa."[2] Visa norms in India are an interesting peephole into the government's concerns and predilections. Taking cover under the shabby old banner of the War on Terror, the Home Ministry has decreed that scholars and academics invited for conferences or seminars require security clearance before they will be given visas. Corporate executives and businessmen do not. So somebody who wants to invest in a dam or build a steel plant or a buy a bauxite mine is not considered a security hazard, whereas a scholar who might wish to participate in a seminar about, say, displacement or communalism, or rising malnutrition in a globalized economy, is. Foreign terrorists with bad intentions have probably guessed by now that they are better off wearing Prada suits and pretending they want to buy a mine than wearing old corduroys and saying they want to attend a seminar. (Some would argue that mine buyers in Prada suits *are* the real terrorists.)

David Barsamian did not travel to India to buy a mine or to attend a conference. He just came to talk to people. The complaint against him, according to "official sources," is that he had reported on events in Jammu and Kashmir during his last visit to India and that these reports were "not based on facts." Remember,

Barsamian is not a reporter, but a journalist who does long-format radio interviews with people, mostly dissidents, about the societies in which they live. Is it illegal for tourists to talk to people in the countries they visit? Would it be illegal for me to travel to the United States or Europe and write about the people I met, even if my writing was "not based on facts"? Who decides which "facts" are correct and which are not? Would Barsamian have been deported if the conversations he recorded had been in praise of the impressive turnouts in Kashmir's elections, instead of about what life is like in the densest military occupation in the world? (Six hundred thousand actively deployed armed personnel for a population of ten million people.)[3] Or if they had been about the army's rescue operations in the 2005 earthquake instead of about the massive unarmed uprisings that took place in three consecutive summers? (And which received no round-the-clock media attention, and no one thought to call "the Kashmir Spring.")

David Barsamian is not the first person to be deported over the Indian government's sensitivities over Kashmir. Professor Richard Shapiro, an anthropologist from San Francisco, was deported from Delhi airport in November 2010 without being given any reason. Most of us believe it was the government's way of punishing his partner Angana Chatterji, a co-convener of the International People's Tribunal on Human Rights and Justice, which first brought international attention to the existence of unmarked mass graves in Kashmir.[4] Earlier this year, on May 28, the outspoken Indian democratic rights activist Gautam Navlakha was deported to Delhi from Srinagar airport. (Farook Abdullah, the former chief minister of Kashmir, justified the deportation, saying that writers like Gautam Navlakha and me had no business entering Kashmir, because "Kashmir is not for burning"—whatever that means.[5]) Kashmir is in the process of being isolated, cut off from the outside world, by two concentric rings of border patrols—in Delhi as well as Srinagar—as though it were already a free country with its own visa regime. Within its borders, of course, it's open season for the government and the army. The art of controlling Kashmiri journalists and ordinary people with a deadly combination of bribes, threats, blackmail, and a whole spectrum of unutterable, carefully crafted cruelties has evolved into an art form.

While the government goes about trying to silence the living, the dead have begun to speak up. It was insensitive of Barsamian to plan a trip to Kashmir just when the State Human Rights Commission was finally shamed into officially acknowledging the existence of twenty-seven hundred unmarked graves from three districts in Kashmir. Reports of thousands of other graves are pouring in from other districts. It is insensitive of the unmarked graves to embarrass the government of India just when India's record is due for review before the UN Human Rights Council.

Apart from Dangerous David, who else is the world's largest democracy afraid of? There's young Lingaram Kodopi, an Adivasi from Dantewada, Chhattisgarh, who was arrested on September 9, 2011.[6] The police say they caught him red-handed in a marketplace while he was handing over protection money from Essar, an iron-ore mining company, to the banned Communist

Party of India (Maoist). His aunt Soni Sori says that he was picked up by plainclothes policemen in a white Bolero from his grandfather's house in Palnar village. Now she's on the run too.[7] Interestingly, even by their own account, the police arrested Lingaram but allowed the Maoists to escape. This is only the latest in a series of bizarre, almost hallucinatory accusations they have made against Lingaram and then withdrawn. His real crime is that he is the *only* journalist who speaks Gondi, the local language, and who knows how to negotiate the remote forest paths in Dantewada, Chhattisgarh, the other war zone in India from which no news must come.

Having signed over vast tracts of indigenous tribal homelands in Central India to multinational mining and infrastructure corporations in a series of secret memorandums of understanding—in complete contravention of the law as well as the Constitution—the government has begun to flood the forests with hundreds of thousands of security forces. All resistance, armed as well as unarmed, has been branded "Maoist." (In Kashmir the preferred phrase is "jihadi elements.") As the civil war grows deadlier, hundreds of villages have been burned to the ground. Thousands of Adivasis have fled as refugees into neighboring states. Hundreds of thousands are living terrified lives hiding in the forests. Paramilitary forces have laid siege to the forest. A network of police informers patrols village bazaars, making trips for essential provisions and medicines a nightmare for villagers. Untold numbers of nameless people are in jail, charged with sedition and waging war on the state, with no lawyers to defend them. Very little news comes out of those forests, and there are no body counts.

So it's not hard to see why young Lingaram Kodopi poses such a threat. Before he trained to become a journalist, he was a driver in Dantewada. In 2009 the police arrested him and confiscated his jeep. For forty days he was locked up in a small toilet, where he was pressured to become a special police officer (SPO) in the Salwa Judum, the government-sponsored vigilante army that was at the time tasked with forcing people to flee from their villages. (The Salwa Judum has since been declared unconstitutional by the Supreme Court.[8]) The police released Lingaram after the Gandhian activist Himanshu Kumar filed a habeas corpus petition in court.[9] But then the police arrested Lingaram's old father and five other members of his family. They attacked his village and warned villagers not to shelter him. Eventually Lingaram escaped to Delhi, where friends and well-wishers got him admission into a journalism school. In April 2010 he traveled to Dantewada and escorted to Delhi the witnesses and victims of the barbarity of the Salwa Judum, the police and paramilitary forces enabling them to give testimony at the Independent People's Tribunal. (In his own testimony Lingaram was sharply critical of the Maoists as well.[10])

That did not deter the Chhattisgarh police. On July 2, 2010, the senior Maoist leader Comrade Azad, official spokesperson for the Maoist Party, was captured and executed by the Andhra Pradesh police.[11] Deputy Inspector General Kalluri of the Chhattisgarh police announced at a press conference that Lingaram Kodopi had been elected by the Maoist Party to take over Comrade Azad's role. (It was like accusing a young schoolchild in 1936 Yenan of being Zhou En Lai.) The charge was met with such derision that the police had to withdraw it.[12] They had also accused Lingaram of being the mastermind of a Maoist attack on a Congress legislator in Dantewada. But perhaps because they had already made themselves look so foolish and vindictive, they decided to bide their time.

Lingaram remained in Delhi, completed his course, and received his diploma in journalism. In March 2011 paramilitary forces burned down three villages in Dantewada—Tadmetla, Timmapuram, and Morapalli.[13] The Chhattisgarh government blamed the Maoists. The Supreme Court assigned the investigation to the Central Bureau of Investigation. Lingaram returned to Dantewada with a video camera and trekked from village to village documenting firsthand testimonies of the villagers, who indicted the police. (You can see some of these on YouTube.)[14] By doing this he made himself one of the most wanted men in Dantewada. On September 9, the police finally got to him.

Lingaram has joined an impressive lineup of troublesome news gatherers and disseminators in Chhattisgarh. Among the earliest to be silenced was the celebrated doctor Binayak Sen, who first raised the alarm about the crimes of the Salwa Judum as far back as 2005. He was arrested in 2007, accused of being a Maoist, and sentenced to life imprisonment. After years in prison, he is out on bail now.[15] Several people followed Binayak Sen into prison—including Piyush Guha and the filmmaker Ajay T.G.[16] Both have been accused of being Maoists. These arrests put a chill into the activists' community in Chhattisgarh but didn't stop some of them from continuing to do what they were doing. Kopa Kunjam worked with Himanshu Kumar's Vansvasi Chetna Ashram, doing exactly what Lingaram tried to do much later—traveling to remote villages, bringing out the news, and carefully documenting the horror that was unfolding. (He was my first guide into the forest villages of Dantewada.) Much of this documentation has made its way into legal cases that are proving to be a source of worry and discomfort to the Chhattisgarh government. In May 2009 the Vansvasi Chetna Ashram, the last neutral shelter for journalists, writers, and academics who were traveling to Dantewada, was demolished by the Chhattisgarh government.[17] In December 2009, on Human Rights Day, Kopa was arrested. He was accused of colluding with the Maoists in the murder of one man and the kidnapping of another.

The case against Kopa has begun to fall apart as the police witnesses, including the man who was kidnapped, have disowned the statements they purportedly made to the police.[18] It doesn't really matter, because in India we all know the process *is* the punishment. It will take years for Kopa to establish his innocence, by which time the administration hopes the arrest will have served its purpose. Many villagers who were encouraged by Kopa to file complaints against the police have been arrested too. Some are in jail. Others have been made to live in roadside camps manned by special police officers (SPOs). That includes many women who committed the crime of being raped. Soon after Kopa's arrest Himanshu Kumar was hounded out of Dantewada. In September 2010 another Adivasi activist, Kartam Joga, was arrested. His offense was to have filed a petition in the Supreme Court in 2007 about the rampant human rights abuses committed by the Salwa Judum. He is being accused of colluding with the Maoists in the April 2010 killing of seventy-six Central Reserve Police personnel in Tadmetla. Kartam Joga is a member of the Communist Party of India (CPI), which has a tense, if not hostile, relationship with the Maoists. Amnesty International has named him a prisoner of conscience.[19]

Meanwhile, the arrests continue at a steady pace. A casual look at the First Information Reports (FIRs) filed by the police give a pretty clear idea of how the deadly business of Due Process works in Dantewada. The texts of many of the FIRs are exactly the same. The name of the accused, the date, the nature of the crime, and the names of witnesses are simply inserted into the biscuit mold. There's nobody to check. Most of those involved, prisoners as well as witnesses, cannot read or write.

One day, in Dantewada too the dead will begin to speak. And it will not just be dead humans, it will be the dead land, dead rivers, dead mountains, and dead creatures in dead forests that will insist on a hearing.

Meanwhile, life goes on. While intrusive surveillance, Internet policing, and phone tapping and the clampdown on those who speak up becomes grimmer with every passing day, it's odd how India is becoming the dream destination of literary festivals. There are about ten of them scheduled over the next few months. Some are funded by the very corporations on whose behalf the police have unleashed their regime of terror. The Harud Literary Festival in Srinagar (postponed for the moment) was slated to be the newest, most exciting one—"as the autumn leaves change colour the valley of Kashmir will resonate with the sound of poetry, literary dialogue, debate and discussions . . ." Its organizers advertised it as an "apolitical" event but did not say how either the rulers or the subjects of a brutal military occupation that has claimed tens of thousands of lives, bereaved thousands of women and children, and maimed a hundred thousand people in its torture chambers can be "apolitical." I wonder—will the literary guests come on tourist visas? Will there be separate ones for Srinagar and Delhi? Will they need security clearance? Will a Kashmiri who speaks out go directly from the festival to an interrogation center, or will she be allowed to go home and change and collect her things? (I'm just being crude here, I know it's more subtle than that.)

The festive din of this spurious freedom helps to muffle the sound of footsteps in airport corridors as the deported are frog-marched onto departing planes, to mute the click of handcuffs locking around strong, warm wrists and the cold metallic clang of prison doors.

Our lungs are gradually being depleted of oxygen. Perhaps it's time to use whatever breath remains in our bodies to say: Open the bloody gates.

SECTION TWO

CHAPTER 4

KASHMIR'S FRUITS OF DISCORD

A week before he was elected in 2008, President Obama said that solving the dispute over Kashmir's struggle for self-determination—which has led to three wars between India and Pakistan since 1947—would be among his "critical tasks."[1] His remarks were greeted with consternation in India, and he has said almost nothing about Kashmir since then.

But on Monday, November 8, 2010, during his visit here, he pleased his hosts immensely by saying the United States would not intervene in Kashmir and announcing his support for India's seat on the UN Security Council.[2] While he spoke eloquently about threats of terrorism, he kept quiet about human rights abuses in Kashmir.

Whether Obama decides to change his position on Kashmir again depends on several factors: how the war in Afghanistan is going, how much help the United States needs from Pakistan, and whether the government of India goes aircraft shopping this winter. (An order for ten Boeing C-17 Globemaster III aircraft, worth $5.8 billion, among other huge business deals in the pipeline, may ensure the president's silence.) But neither Obama's silence nor his intervention is likely to make the people in Kashmir drop the stones in their hands.

I was in Kashmir ten days ago, in that beautiful valley on the Pakistani border, home to three great civilizations—Islamic, Hindu, and Buddhist. It's a valley of myth and history. Some believe that Jesus died there, others that Moses went there to find the Lost Tribe. Millions worship at the Hazratbal shrine, where a few days a year a hair of the Prophet Muhammad is displayed to believers.

Now Kashmir, caught between the influence of militant Islam from Pakistan and Afghanistan, America's interests in the region, and Indian nationalism (which is becoming increasingly aggressive and "Hinduized"), is considered a nuclear flash point. It is patrolled by more than 500,000 soldiers and has become the most highly militarized zone in the world.

The atmosphere on the highway between Kashmir's capital, Srinagar, and my destination, the little apple town of Shopian in the South, was tense. Groups of soldiers were deployed along the highway, in the orchards, in the fields, on the rooftops, and outside shops in the little market squares. Despite months of curfew, the "stone pelters" calling for *azadi* (freedom), inspired by the Palestinian intifada, were out again. Some stretches of the highway were covered with so many of these stones that you needed an SUV to drive over them.

Fortunately the friends I was with knew alternative routes down the back lanes and village roads. The "long cut" gave me the time to listen to their stories of this year's uprising. The youngest, still a boy, told us that when three of his friends were arrested for throwing stones, the police pulled out their fingernails—every nail, on both hands.

For three years in a row now, Kashmiris have been in the streets protesting what they see as India's violent occupation. But the militant uprising against the Indian government that began with the support of Pakistan twenty years ago is in retreat. The Indian army estimates that there are fewer than five hundred militants operating in the Kashmir Valley today. The war has left seventy thousand dead and tens of thousands debilitated by torture. Many, many thousands have "disappeared." More than 200,000 Kashmiri Hindus have fled the valley. Though the number of militants has come down, the number of Indian soldiers deployed remains undiminished.

But India's military domination ought not to be confused with a political victory. Ordinary people armed with nothing but their fury have risen up against the Indian security forces. A whole generation of young people who have grown up in a grid of checkpoints, bunkers, army camps, and interrogation centers, whose childhood was spent witnessing "catch and kill" operations, whose imaginations are imbued with spies, informers, "unidentified gunmen," intelligence operatives, and rigged elections, has lost its patience as well as its fear. With an almost mad courage, Kashmir's young have faced down armed soldiers and taken back their streets.

Since April, when the army killed three civilians and then passed them off as "terrorists," masked stone throwers, most of them students, have brought life in Kashmir to a grinding halt.

The Indian government has retaliated with bullets, curfew, and censorship. Just in the last few months, 111 people have been killed, most of them teenagers; more than 3,000 have been wounded and 1,000 arrested.

But still they come out, the young, and throw stones. They don't seem to have leaders or belong to a political party. They represent themselves. And suddenly the second-largest standing army in the world doesn't quite know what to do. The Indian government doesn't know with whom to negotiate. And many Indians are slowly realizing they have been lied to for decades. The once solid consensus on Kashmir suddenly seems a little fragile.

I was in a bit of trouble the morning we drove to Shopian. A few days earlier, at a public meeting in Delhi, I said that Kashmir was disputed territory and, contrary to the Indian government's claims, it couldn't be called an "integral" part of India. Outraged politicians and news anchors demanded that I be arrested for sedition. The government, terrified of being seen as "soft," issued threatening statements, and the situation escalated. Day after day, on prime-time news, I was being called a traitor, a white-collar terrorist, and several other names reserved for insubordinate women. But sitting in that car on the road to Shopian, listening to my friends, I could not bring myself to regret what I had said in Delhi.

We were on our way to visit a man called Shakeel Ahmed Ahangar. The previous day he had come all the way to Srinagar, where I had been staying, to press me, with an urgency that was hard to ignore, to visit Shopian.

I first met Shakeel in June 2009, only a few weeks after the bodies of Nilofar, his twenty-two-year-old wife, and Asiya, his seventeen-year-old sister, were found lying a thousand yards apart in a shallow stream in a high-security zone—a floodlit area between army and state police camps. The first postmortem report confirmed rape and murder. But then the system kicked in. New autopsy reports overturned the initial findings, and after the ugly business of exhuming the bodies, rape was ruled out. It was declared that in both cases the cause of death was drowning.[3] Protests shut Shopian down for forty-seven days, and the valley was convulsed with anger for months. Eventually it looked as though the Indian government had managed to defuse the crisis. But the anger over the killings has magnified the intensity of this year's uprising.

Shakeel wanted us to visit him in Shopian because he was being threatened by the police for speaking out, and he hoped our visit would demonstrate that people even outside of Kashmir were looking out for him, that he was not alone.

It was apple season in Kashmir, and as we approached Shopian we could see families in their orchards, busily packing apples into wooden crates in the slanting afternoon light. I worried that a couple of the little red-cheeked children who looked so much like apples themselves might be crated by mistake. The news of our visit had preceded us, and a small knot of people were waiting on the road.

Shakeel's house is on the edge of the graveyard where his wife and sister are buried. It was dark by the time we arrived, and there was a power failure. We sat in a semicircle around a lantern and listened to him tell the story we all knew so well. Other people entered the room. Other terrible stories poured out, ones that are not in human rights reports, stories about what happens to women who live in remote villages where there are more soldiers than civilians. Shakeel's young son tumbled around in the darkness, moving from lap to lap. "Soon he'll be old enough to understand what happened to his mother," Shakeel said more than once.

Just when we rose to leave, a messenger arrived to say that Shakeel's father-in-law—Nilofar's father—was expecting us at his home. We sent our regrets; it was late and if we stayed longer it would be unsafe for us to drive back.

Minutes after we said goodbye and crammed ourselves into the car, a friend's phone rang. It was a journalist colleague of his with news for me: "The police are typing up the warrant. She's going to be arrested tonight." We drove in silence for a while, past truck after truck being loaded with apples. "It's unlikely," my friend said finally. "It's just psy-ops."

But then, as we picked up speed on the highway, we were overtaken by a car full of men waving us down. Two men on a motorcycle asked our driver to pull over. I steeled myself for what was coming. A man appeared at the car window. He had slanting emerald eyes and a salt-and-pepper beard that went halfway down his chest. He introduced himself as Abdul Hai, father of the murdered Nilofar.

"How could I let you go without your apples?" he said. The bikers started loading two crates of apples into the back of our car.

Then Abdul Hai reached into a pocket of his worn brown cloak and brought out an egg. He placed it in my palm and folded my fingers over it. And then he placed another in my other hand. The eggs were still warm. "God bless and keep you," he said, and walked away into the dark. What greater reward could a writer want?

I wasn't arrested that night. Instead, in what is becoming a common political strategy, officials outsourced their displeasure to the mob. A few days after I returned home, the women's wing of the Bharatiya Janata Party (the right-wing Hindu nationalist opposition) staged a demonstration outside my house, calling for my arrest. Television vans arrived in advance to broadcast the event live. The murderous Bajrang Dal, a militant Hindu group that in 2002 spearheaded attacks against Muslims in Gujarat in which more than a thousand people were killed, have announced that they are going to "teach me a lesson" with all the means at their disposal, including by filing criminal charges against me in different courts across the country.[4]

Indian nationalists and the government seem to believe that they can fortify their idea of a resurgent India with a combination of bullying and Boeing airplanes. But they don't understand the subversive strength of warm boiled eggs.

CHAPTER 5

A PERFECT DAY FOR DEMOCRACY

Wasn't it? Yesterday I mean. Spring announced itself in Delhi. The sun was out, and the Law took its Course. Just before breakfast, Afzal Guru, prime accused in the 2001 Parliament Attack, was secretly hanged, and his body was interred in Tihar Jail.[1] Was he buried next to Maqbool Butt? (The other Kashmiri who was hanged in Tihar in 1984. Kashmiris will mark that anniversary tomorrow.) Afzal's wife and son were not informed. "The Authorities intimated the family through Speed Post and Registered Post," the home secretary told the press; "the Director General of J&K Police has been told to check whether they got it or not."[2] No big deal, they're only the family of a Kash miri terrorist.

In a moment of rare unity the Nation, or at least its major political parties, the Congress, the BJP, and the CPM, came together as one (barring a few squabbles about "delay" and "timing") to celebrate the triumph of the Rule of Law. The Conscience of the Nation, which broadcasts live from TV studios these days, unleashed its collective intellect on us—the usual cocktail of papal passion and a delicate grip on facts. Even though the man was dead and gone, like cowards that hunt in packs, they seemed to need each other to keep their courage up. Perhaps because deep inside themselves they know that they all colluded to do something terribly wrong.

What are the facts?

On December 13, 2001, five armed men drove through the gates of the Parliament House in a white Ambassador fitted out with an improvised explosive device (IED). When they were challenged they jumped out of the car and opened fire. They killed eight security personnel and a gardener. In the gun battle that followed all five attackers were killed. In one of the many versions of confessions Afzal Guru made in police custody he identified the men as Mohammed, Rana, Raja, Hamza, and Haider. That's all we know about them even today. L. K. Advani, the then home minister, said they "looked like Pakistanis." (He should know what Pakistanis look like, right? Being a Sindhi himself.) Based *only* on Afzal's confession (which the Supreme Court subsequently set aside, citing "lapses" and "violations of procedural safeguards"), the government of India recalled its ambassador from Pakistan and mobilized half a million soldiers to the Pakistan border. There was talk of nuclear war. Foreign embassies issued travel advisories and evacuated their staff from Delhi. The standoff lasted for months and cost India thousands of crores.

On December 14, 2001, the Delhi Police Special Cell claimed it had cracked the case. On December 15 it arrested the "mastermind," Professor S. A. R. Geelani, in Delhi and Showkat Guru and Afzal Guru in a fruit market in Srinagar.[3] Subsequently they arrested Afsan Guru, Showkat's wife. The media enthusiastically disseminated the Special Cell's version. These were some of the headlines: "DU Lecturer Was Terror Plan Hub," "Varsity Don Guided Fidayeen," "Don Lectured on Terror in Free Time." Zee TV broadcast a "docudrama" called *December 13th*, a re-creation that claimed to be the "Truth Based on the Police Charge Sheet." (If the police version is the truth, then why have courts?) Then Prime Minister Vajpayee and L. K. Advani publicly appreciated the film. The Supreme Court refused to stay the screening, saying that the media would not influence judges. The film was broadcast only a few days before the fast-track court sentenced Afzal, Showkat, and Geelani to death. Subsequently the High Court acquitted the "mastermind," Geelani, and Afsan Guru. The Supreme Court upheld the acquittal. But in its August 5, 2005, judgment it gave Mohammed Afzal three life sentences and a double death sentence.

Contrary to the lies that have been put about by some senior journalists who would have known better, Afzal Guru was not one of "the terrorists who stormed Parliament House on December 13th 2001," nor was he among those who "opened fire on security personnel, apparently killing three of the six who died." (That was the BJP Rajya Sabha MP, Chandan Mitra, in the *Pioneer*, October 7, 2006.) Even the police charge sheet does not accuse him of that. The Supreme Court judgment says the evidence is circumstantial: "As is the case with most conspiracies, there is and could be no direct evidence amounting to criminal conspiracy." But then it goes on to say: "The incident, which resulted in heavy casualties had shaken the entire nation, and the collective conscience of society will only be satisfied if capital punishment is awarded to the offender."[4]

Who crafted our collective conscience on the Parliament Attack case? Could it have been the facts we gleaned in the papers? The films we saw on TV?

There are those who will argue that the very fact that the courts acquitted S. A. R. Geelani and convicted Afzal proves that the trial was free and fair. Was it?

The trial in the fast-track court began in May 2002. The world was still convulsed by post-9/11 frenzy. The US government was gloating prematurely over its "victory" in Afghanistan. The Gujarat pogrom was ongoing. And in the Parliament Attack case, the Law was indeed taking its own course. At the most crucial stage of a criminal case, when evidence is presented, when witnesses are cross-examined, when the foundations of the argument are laid—in the High Court and Supreme Court you can only argue points of law, you cannot introduce new evidence—Afzal Guru, locked in a high-security solitary cell, had no lawyer. The court-appointed junior lawyer did not visit his client even once in jail; he did not summon any witnesses in Afzal's defense and did not cross-examine the prosecution witnesses. The judge expressed his inability to do anything about the situation.

Even still, from the word go, the case fell apart. A few examples out of many:

How did the police get to Afzal? They said that S. A. R. Geelani led them to him. But the court records show that the message to arrest Afzal went out before they picked up Geelani. The High Court called this a "material contradiction" but left it at that.

The two most incriminating pieces of evidence against Afzal were a cell phone and a laptop confiscated at the time of arrest. The Arrest Memos were signed by Bismillah, Geelani's brother, in Delhi. The Seizure Memos were signed by two men of the J&K Police, one of them an old tormentor from Afzal's past as a surrendered "militant." The computer and cell phone were not sealed, as evidence is required to be. During the trial it emerged that the hard disk of the laptop had been accessed after the arrest. It contained only the fake Home Ministry passes and the fake identity cards that the "terrorists" used to access Parliament. And a Zee TV video clip of Parliament House. So according to the police, Afzal had deleted all the information except the most incriminating bits, and he was speeding off to hand it over to Ghazi Baba, whom the charge sheet described as the chief of operations.

A witness for the prosecution, Kamal Kishore, identified Afzal and told the court he had sold him the crucial SIM card that connected all the accused in the case to each other on December 4, 2001. But the prosecution's own call records showed that the SIM was actually operational from November 6, 2001.

It goes on and on, this pile-up of lies and fabricated evidence. The courts note them, but for their pains the police get no more than a gentle rap on their knuckles. Nothing more.

Then there's the backstory. Like most surrendered militants, Afzal was easy meat in Kashmir—a victim of torture, blackmail, extortion. In the larger scheme of things he was a nobody. Anyone who was really interested in solving the mystery of the Parliament Attack would have followed the dense trail of evidence that was on offer. No one did, thereby ensuring that the real authors of conspiracy will remain unidentified and uninvestigated.

Now that Afzal Guru has been hanged, I hope our collective conscience has been satisfied. Or is our cup of blood still only half full?

CHAPTER 6

CONSEQUENCES OF HANGING AFZAL GURU

What are the political consequences of the secret and sudden hanging of Mohammad Afzal Guru, prime accused in the 2001 Parliament Attack, going to be? Does anybody know?

The memo, in callous bureaucratese, with every name insultingly misspelled, sent by the superintendent of Central Jail Number 3, Tihar, New Delhi, to "Mrs Tabassum w/o Sh Afjal Guru," reads:

> The mercy petition of Sh Mohd Afjal Guru s/o Habibillah has been rejected by Hon'ble President of India. Hence the execution of Mohd Afjal Guru s/o Habibillah has been fixed for 09/02/2013 at 8 AM in Central Jail No-3.
>
> This is for your information and for further necessary action.

The memo arrived after the execution had already taken place, denying Tabassum one last legal chance—the right to challenge the rejection of the mercy petition.[1] Both Afzal *and* his family, separately, had that right. Both were thwarted. Even though it is mandatory in law, the memo to Tabassum provided no reason for the president's rejection of the mercy petition. If no reason is given, on what basis do you appeal? All the other prisoners on death row in India have been given that last chance.

Since Tabassum was not allowed to meet with her husband before he was hanged, since her son was not allowed to get a few last words of advice from his father, since she was not given his body to bury, and since there can be no funeral, what "further necessary action" does the Jail Manual prescribe? Anger? Wild, irreparable grief? Unquestioning acceptance? Complete integration?

After the hanging, there were unseemly celebrations on the streets. The bereaved wives of the people who were killed in the Attack were displayed on TV, with chairman of the All-India Anti-Terrorist Front M. S. Bitta and his ferocious mustaches playing the CEO of their sad little company. Will anybody tell them that the men who shot their husbands were killed at the same time, in the same place, right there and then? And that those who planned the Attack will never be brought to justice because we still don't know who they are?

Meanwhile Kashmir is under curfew, once again. Its people have been locked down like cattle in a pen, once again. They have defied the curfew, once again. Three people have already been killed in three days, and fifteen more grievously injured.[2] Newspapers have been shut down, but anybody who trawls the Internet will see that this time the rage of young Kashmiris is not defiant and exuberant as it was during the mass uprisings in the summers of 2008, 2009, and 2010—even though 180 people lost their lives on those occasions. This time the anger is cold and corrosive. Unforgiving. Is there any reason why it shouldn't be?

For more than twenty years Kashmiris have endured a military occupation. The tens of thousands who lost their lives were killed in prisons, in torture centers, and in "encounters," genuine as well as fake. What sets the execution of Afzal Guru apart is that it has given the young, who have never had any firsthand experience of democracy, a ringside seat to watch the full majesty of Indian democracy at work. They have watched the wheels turning, they have seen all its hoary institutions, the government, police, courts, political parties, and yes, the media, collude to hang a man, a Kashmiri, whom they do not believe to have received a fair trial, and whose guilt was by no means established beyond reasonable doubt. (He went virtually unrepresented in the lower court during the most crucial stage of the trial. Not only did the state-appointed counsel never visit his client in prison, he actually admitted incriminating evidence against him. The Supreme Court deliberated on that matter and decided it was okay.)[3] They have watched the government pull him out of the death row queue and execute him out of turn. What direction, what form will their new cold, corrosive anger take? Will it lead them to the blessed liberation they so yearn for and have sacrificed a whole generation for, or will it lead to yet another cycle of cataclysmic violence, of being beaten down and then having "normalcy" imposed on them under soldiers' boots?

All of us who live in the region know that 2014 is going to be a watershed year. There will be elections in Pakistan, in India, and in the state of Jammu and Kashmir. We know that when the United States withdraws its troops from Afghanistan, the chaos from an already seriously destabilized Pakistan will spill into Kashmir, as it has done before. By executing Afzal Guru in the way that it did, the government of India has taken a decision to fuel that process of destabilization, to actually invite it in. (As it did before, by rigging the 1987 elections in Kashmir.) After three consecutive years of mass protests in the valley ended in 2010, the government invested a great deal in restoring its version of "normalcy" (happy tourists, voting Kashmiris). The question is, why was it willing to reverse all its own efforts? Leaving aside issues of the legality, the morality, and the venality of executing Afzal Guru in the way that it did, and looking at it just politically, tactically, it is a dangerous and irresponsible thing to have done. But it was done. Clearly, and knowingly. *Why?*

I used the word *irresponsible* advisedly. Look what happened the last time around.

In 2001, within a week of the Parliament Attack (and a few days after Afzal Guru's arrest), the government recalled its ambassador from Pakistan and dispatched half a million troops to the border. On what basis was that done? The only thing the public was told is that while Afzal Guru was in the custody of the Delhi Police Special Cell, he had admitted to being a member of the Pakistan-based militant group Jaish-e-Mohammed (JeM). The Supreme Court set aside that "confession" extracted in police custody as inadmissible in law.[4] Does a document that is inadmissible in law become admissible in war?

In its final judgment on the case, apart from the now famous statements about "satisfying collective conscience" and having no direct evidence, the Supreme Court also said there was "no evidence that Mohammed Afzal belonged to any terrorist group or organization."[5] So what justified that military aggression, that loss of soldiers' lives, that massive hemorrhaging of public money, and the real risk of nuclear war? (Remember how foreign embassies issued travel advisories and evacuated their staff?) Was there some intelligence that preceded the Parliament Attack and the arrest of Afzal Guru that we had not been told about? If so, how could the Attack have been allowed to happen? And if the intelligence was accurate enough to justify such dangerous military posturing, don't people in India, Pakistan, and Kashmir have the right to know what it was? Why was that evidence not produced in court to establish Afzal Guru's guilt?

In the endless debates around the Parliament Attack case, on this, perhaps the most crucial issue of all, there has been dead silence from all quarters—leftists, rightists, Hindutva-ists, secularists, nationalists, seditionists, cynics, critics. Why?

Maybe the JeM *did* mastermind the Attack. Praveen Swami, perhaps the Indian media's best-known expert on "terrorism," who seems to have enviable sources in the Indian police and intelligence agencies, has recently cited the 2003 testimony of former ISI Chief Lieutenant General Javed Ashraf Qazi and the 2004 book by Muhammad Amir Rana, a Pakistani scholar, holding the JeM responsible for the Parliament Attack.[6] (This belief in the veracity of the testimony of the chief of an organization whose mandate it is to destabilize India is touching.) It still doesn't explain what evidence there was in 2001, when the army mobilization took place.

For the sake of argument, let's accept that the JeM carried out the Attack. Maybe the ISI was involved too. We needn't pretend that the government of Pakistan is innocent of carrying out covert activity over Kashmir. (Just as the government of India does in Balochistan and parts of Pakistan. Remember the Indian army trained the Mukti Bahini in East Pakistan in the 1970s. It trained six different Srilankan Tamil militant groups, including the LTTE, in the 1980s.)

It's a filthy scenario all around.

What would a war with Pakistan have achieved then, and what will it achieve now? (Apart from a massive loss of life. And fattening the bank accounts of some arms dealers.) Indian hawks routinely suggest the only way to "root out the problem" is "hot pursuit" and the "taking out" of "terrorist camps" in Pakistan. Really? It would be interesting to research how many of the aggressive strategic experts and defense analysts on our TV screens have an interest in the defense and weapons industry. They don't even need war. They just need a warlike climate in which military spending remains on an upward graph. This idea of hot pursuit is even stupider and more pathetic than it sounds. What would they bomb? A few individuals? Their barracks and food supplies? Or their ideology? Look how the US government's "hot pursuit" has ended in Afghanistan. And look how a "security grid" of half a million soldiers has not been able to subdue the unarmed civilian population of Kashmir. And India is going to cross international borders to bomb a country—with nuclear arms—that is rapidly devolving into chaos? India's professional warmongers derive a great deal of satisfaction from sneering at what they see as the disintegration of Pakistan. Anyone with a rudimentary working knowledge of history and geography would know that the breakdown of Pakistan (into a gangland of crazed, nihilistic religious zealots) is absolutely no reason for anyone to rejoice.

The US presence in Afghanistan and Iraq, and Pakistan's official role as America's junior partner in the War on Terror, makes that region a much-reported place. The rest of the world is at least aware of the dangers unfolding there. Less understood, and harder to read, is the perilous wind that's picking up speed in the world's favorite new superpower. The Indian economy is in considerable trouble. The aggressive, acquisitive ambition that economic liberalization unleashed in the newly created middle class is quickly turning into an equally aggressive frustration. The aircraft they were sitting in has begun to stall just after takeoff. Exhilaration is turning to panic.

The General Election is due in 2014. Even without an exit poll, I can tell you what the results will be. Though it may not be obvious to the naked eye, once again we will have a Congress–Bharatiya Janata Party (BJP) coalition. (Two parties, each with a mass murder of thousands of people belonging to minority communities under their belts.) The Communist Party of India–Marxist (CPI-M) will give support from outside, even though it hasn't been asked to. Oh, and it will be a Strong State. (On the hanging front, the gloves are already off. Could the next in line be Balwant Singh Rajoana, on death row for the assassination of Punjab's chief minister Beant Singh? His execution could revive Khalistani sentiment in the Punjab and put the Akali Dal and the BJP on the mat. Perfect old-style Congress politics.)[7]

But that old-style politics is in some difficulty. In the last few turbulent months, it is not just the image of major political parties but politics itself, the idea of politics as we know it, that has taken a battering. Again and again, whether it's about corruption, rising prices, or rape and the rising violence against women, the new, emerging middle class is at the barricades. They can be water-cannoned or lathi-charged, but they cannot be shot and imprisoned in their thousands, in the way the poor can, in the way Dalits, Adivasis, Muslims, Kashmiris, Nagas, and Manipuris can—and have been. The old political parties know that if there is not to be a complete meltdown, this aggression has to be headed off, redirected. They know that they must work together to bring politics back to what it *used* to be. What better way than a communal conflagration? (How else can the secular play at being secular and the communal be communal?) Maybe even a little war, so that we can play Hawks and Doves all over again.

What better solution than to aim a kick at that tried and trusted old political football—Kashmir? The hanging of Afzal Guru, its brazenness and timing, is deliberate.[8] It has brought politics and anger back onto Kashmir's streets.

India hopes to manage it with the usual combination of brute force and poisonous Machiavellian manipulation designed to pit people against one another. The war in Kashmir is presented to the world as a battle between an inclusive secular democracy and radical Islamists. What then should we make of the fact that Mufti Bashiruddin, the so-called Grand Mufti of Kashmir (which, by the way, is a completely phantom post)—who has made the most abominable hate speeches and has issued fatwah after fatwah, intended to present Kashmir as a demonic, monolithic Wahabi society—is actually a government-anointed cleric? Kids on Facebook will be arrested, but never he.[9] What should we make of the fact that the Indian government looks away while money from Saudi Arabia (that most steadfast partner of the United States) is pouring into Kashmir's madrassas? How different is this from what the CIA did in Afghanistan all those years ago? That whole sorry business created Osama Bin Laden, Al Qaeda, and the Taliban. It has decimated Afghanistan and Pakistan. What sort of incubus will this unleash?

The old political football is not going to be all that easy to control. And it's radioactive. A few days ago Pakistan tested a short-range battlefield nuclear missile to protect itself against threats from "evolving scenarios." Two weeks ago the Kashmir police published "survival tips" for nuclear war. Apart from advising people to build toilet-equipped bombproof basements large enough to house their entire families for two weeks, it said: "During a nuclear attack, motorists should dive out of their cars toward the blast to save themselves from being crushed by their soon-to-be tumbling vehicles." And it warned everyone to "expect some initial disorientation as the blast wave may blow down and carry away many prominent and familiar features."[10]

Prominent and familiar features may have already blown down.

Perhaps we should all jump out of our soon-to-be-tumbling vehicles.

AFTERWORD

SPEECH TO THE PEOPLE'S UNIVERSITY

Yesterday morning the police cleared Zuccotti Park, but today the people are back. The police should know that this protest is not a battle for territory. We're not fighting for the right to occupy a park here or there. We are fighting for Justice. Justice, not just for the people of the United States, but for everybody. What you have achieved since September 17, when the Occupy Movement began in the United States, is to introduce a new imagination, a new political language, into the heart of Empire. You have reintroduced the right to dream into a system that tried to turn everybody into zombies mesmerized into equating mindless consumerism with happiness and fulfillment. As a writer, let me tell you, this is an immense achievement. I cannot thank you enough.

We were talking about justice. Today, as we speak, the army of the United States is waging a war of occupation in Iraq and Afghanistan. US drones are killing civilians in Pakistan and beyond. Tens of thousands of US troops and death squads are moving into Africa. If spending trillions of dollars of your money to administer occupations in Iraq and Afghanistan is not enough, a war against Iran is being talked up. Ever since the Great Depression, the manufacture of weapons and the export of war have been key ways in which the United States has stimulated its economy. Just recently, under President Obama, the United States made a sixty-billion-dollar arms deal with Saudi Arabia.[1] It hopes to sell thousands of bunker busters to the United Arab Emirates. It has sold five billion dollars' worth of military aircraft to my country, India—my country, which has more poor people than all the poorest countries of Africa put together.[2] All these wars, from the bombing of Hiroshima and Nagasaki to Vietnam, Korea, Latin America, have claimed millions of lives—all of them fought to secure "the American way of life."

Today we know that "the American way of life"—the model that the rest of the world is meant to aspire toward—has resulted in four hundred people owning the wealth of half of the population of the United States. It has meant thousands of people being turned out of their homes and jobs while the US government bailed out banks and corporations—American International Group (AIG) alone was given 182 billion dollars.

The Indian government worships US economic policy. As a result of twenty years of the Free Market economy, today one hundred of India's richest people own assets worth one-fourth of the country's GDP while more than 80 percent of the people live on less than fifty cents a day.[3] Two hundred fifty thousand farmers driven into a spiral of death have committed suicide.[4] We call this progress and now think of ourselves as a superpower. Like you, we are well qualified, we have nuclear bombs and obscene inequality.

The good news is that people have had enough and are not going to take it anymore. The Occupy Movement has joined thousands of other resistance movements all over the world in which the poorest of people are standing up and stopping the richest corporations in their tracks. Few of us dreamed that we would see you, the people of the United States, on our side, trying to do this in the heart of Empire. I don't know how to communicate the enormity of what this means.

They (the 1%) say that we don't have demands . . . they don't know, perhaps, that our anger alone would be enough to destroy them. But here are some things—a few "pre-revolutionary" thoughts I had—for us to think about together.

We want to put a lid on this system that manufactures inequality.

We want to put a cap on the unfettered accumulation of wealth and property by individuals as well as corporations.

As cap-ists and lid-ites, we demand:

One: An end to cross-ownership in businesses. For example: weapons manufacturers cannot own TV stations, mining corporations cannot run newspapers, business houses cannot fund universities, drug companies cannot control public health funds.

Two: Natural resources and essential infrastructure—water supply, electricity, health, and education—cannot be privatized.

Three: Everybody must have the right to shelter, education, and health care.

Four: The children of the rich cannot inherit their parents' wealth.

This struggle has reawakened our imagination. Somewhere along the way, Capitalism reduced the idea of justice to mean just "human rights," and the idea of dreaming of equality became blasphemous. We are not fighting to tinker with reforming a system that needs to be replaced.

As a cap-ist and a lid-ite, I salute your struggle.

Salaam and Zindabad.

NOTES

1. Pablo Neruda, "The Judges," in *The Poetry of Pablo Neruda*, ed. Ilan Stavans (New York: Farrar, Straus and Giroux, 2003), 229.

PREFACE: THE PRESIDENT TOOK THE SALUTE

1. "Migrants Blamed for Surging Crimes in Cities," *Indian Express*, April 2, 2013, http://newindianexpress.com/nation/Migrants-blamed-for-surging-crimes-in-Delhi/2013/04/22/article1555785.ece.

CHAPTER 1: CAPITALISM: A GHOST STORY

1. "Mukesh Ambani Tops for the Third Year as India's Richest," *Forbes Asia*, news release, September 30, 2010. The article notes, "The combined net worth of India's 100 richest people is $300 billion, up from $276 billion last year. This year, there are 69 billionaires on the India Rich List, 17 more than last year." India's 2009 GDP was $1.2 trillion.
2. Vikas Bajaj, "For Wealthy Indian Family, Palatial House Is No Home," *New York Times*, October 18, 2011, http://www.nytimes.com/2011/10/19/business/global/this-luxurious-house-is-not-a-home.html.
3. Frederick Engels and Karl Marx, *Manifesto of the Communist Party*, trans. Samel Moore (Torfaen, UK: Merlin, 1998), 17.

4. P. Sainath, "Farm Suicides Rise in Maharashtra, State Still Leads the List," *Hindu*, July 3, 2012, www.thehindu.com/opinion/columns/sainath/article3595351.ece.
5. National Commission for Enterprises in the Unorganised Sector (NCEUS), *Report on Conditions of Work and Promotion of Livelihoods in the Unorganised Sector*, Government of India, August 2007. The state-supported study notes that though a "buoyancy in the economy did lead to a sense of euphoria by the turn of the last century . . . a majority of the people . . . were not touched by this euphoria. At the end of 2004–5, about 836 million or 77 per cent of the population were living below Rs.20 a day and constituted most of India's informal economy" (1).
6. As of March 2013, Mukesh Ambani was worth $21.5 billion, according to a Forbes profile: http://www.forbes.com/profile/mukesh-ambani/.
7. "RIL Buys 95% Stake in Infotel Broadband," *Times of India*, June 11, 2010, http://articles.timesofindia.indiatimes.com/2010-06-11/telecom/28277245_1_infotel-broadband-broadband-wireless-access-spectrum-world-class-consumer-experiences.
8. Depali Gupta, "Mukesh Ambani–Owned Infotel Broadband to Set Up over 1,000,000 Towers for 4G Operations," *Economic Times*, August 23, 2012, http://articles.economictimes.indiatimes.com/2012-04-23/news/31387124_1_telecom-towers-largest-tower-tower-arm.
9. Brinda Karat, "Of Mines, Minerals and Tribal Rights," *Hindu*, May 15, 2012, http://www.thehindu.com/opinion/lead/of-mines-minerals-and-tribal-rights/article3419034.ece.
10. See Michael Levien, "The Land Question: Special Economic Zones and the Political Economy of Dispossession in India," *Journal of Peasant Studies* 39, nos. 3–4 (2012): 933–69.
11. S. Sakthivel and Pinaki Joddar, "Unorganised Sector Workforce in India: Trends, Patterns and Social Security Coverage," *Economic and Political Weekly*, May 27, 2006, 2107–14.

12. "India Approves Increase in Royalties on Mineral Mining," *Wall Street Journal*, August 12, 2009, http://online.wsj.com/article/SB125006823591525437.html.
13. From a 2009 Ministry of Rural Development report titled "State Agrarian Relations and Unfinished Task of Land Reforms," commissioned by the Government of India: "The new approach came about with the *Salwa Judum*. . . . [Its] first financiers . . were Tata and the Essar. . . . 640 villages as per official statistics were laid bare, burnt to the ground and emptied with the force of the gun and the blessings of the state. 350,000 tribals, half the total population of Dantewada district are displaced, their womenfolk raped, their daughters killed, and their youth maimed. Those who could not escape into the jungle were herded together into refugee camps run and managed by the *Salwa Judum*. Others continue to hide in the forest or have migrated to the nearby tribal tracts in Maharashtra, Andhra Pradesh and Orissa. 640 villages are empty. Villages sitting on tons of iron ore are effectively de-peopled and available for the highest bidder. The latest information that is being circulated is that both Essar Steel and Tata Steel are willing to take over the empty landscape and manage the mines" (161). http://www.rd.ap.gov.in/IKPLand/MRD_Committee_Report_V_01_Mar_09.pdf.
14. P. Pradhan, "Police Firing at Kalinganagar," People's Union for Civil Liberties (PUCL) report, Orissa. April 2006.
15. Ibid.
16. Sudha Ramachandran, "India's War on Maoists under Attack," *Asia Times Online*, May 26, 2010, http://www.atimes.com/atimes/South_Asia/LE26Df02.html.
17. "Anti-Naxal Operations: Gov't to Deplot 10,000 CRPF Troopers," *Zeenews.com*, October 30, 2012, http://zeenews.india.com/news/nation/anti-naxal-operations-govt-to-deploy-10-000-crpf-troopers_808442.html. See also http://www.indiandefence.com/

forums/national-politics/22342-kanwar-yet-again-urges-army-action-naxals.html; http://news.webindia123.com/news/Articles/India/20121115/2102012.html; http://articles.timesofindia.indiatimes.com/2012-06-02/india/31983397_1_s-vireesh-prabhu-gadchiroli-naxals.

18. See Human Rights Watch, "Getting Away with Murder: 50 Years of the Armed Forces Special Powers Act (AFSPA)," August 2008. The report states that AFSPA's ability to act "on suspicion" has led to thousands of disappearances in Jammu and Kashmir. Many of those who've disappeared are believed to be in "unmarked graves that security forces say are the burials of unidentified militants. Human rights groups have long called for an independent investigation and forensic tests to establish the identity of those in the graves, but the government has yet to respond to that demand" (12).
19. J. Balaji, "Soni Sori Case: HRW Wants PM to Order Impartial Probe on Torture," *Hindu*, March 8, 2011, http://www.thehindu.com/news/states/soni-sori-case-hrw-wants-pm-to-order-impartial-probe-on-torture/article2971330.ece?ref=relatedNews. Although Soni Sori has been acquitted in six of the eight cases filed against her, she remains in a Chhattisgarh jail. See Suvojit Bagchi, "Soni Sori Acquitted in a Case of Attack on Congress Leader," *Hindu*, May 1, 2013, http://www.thehindu.com/news/national/soni-sori-kodopi-acquitted-of-murder-charges/article4673791.ece.
20. Aman Sethi, "High Court Stays Clearance for DB Power Coal Mine in Chhattisgarh," *Hindu*, December 12, 2001, http://www.thehindu.com/todays-paper/tp-national/high-court-stays-clearance-for-db-power-coal-mine-in-chhattisgarh/article2707597.ece.
21. Sanjib Kr Baruah, "Dam Wrong," *Hindustan Times*, September 2, 2010, http://www.hindustantimes.com/News-Feed/Travel/Dam-wrong/Article1-604611.aspx.
22. "Kashmir Power Cut Protest Turns Deadly," *Aljazeera*, January 3,

2012, http://www.aljazeera.com/news/asia/2012/01/201212181142597804.html.

23. "Report Raised Fears about Proximity of Kalpasar Dam and Mithivirdi N-Project," *Indian Express*, May 3, 2013, http://www.indianexpress.com/news/-report-raised-fears-about-proximity-of-kalpsar-dam---mithivirdi-nproject-/1110913/.
24. Vinod K. Jose, "The Emperor Uncrowned: The Rise of Narendra Modi," *Caravan Magazine*, March 1, 2012, http://www.caravanmagazine.in/print/1006.
25. See http://www.investindholera.com/DMIC-projects.html.
26. Maj. Gen. Dhruv Katoch et al., "Perception Management of the Indian Army," Centre for Land Warfare Studies seminar, Delhi, February 21, 2012, http://www.claws.in/index.php?action=master&task=1092&u_id=36.
27. Lydia Polgreen, "High Ideals and Corruption Dominate Think Festival Agenda," *New York Times*, November 1, 2011, http://india.blogs.nytimes.com/2011/11/11/high-ideals-and-corruption-dominate-think-festival-agenda/. While Tehelka held a "Summit of the Powerless" conference in 2006, initiating discussions of Naxalism and farmer suicides, the 2011 Think Fest, hosted by the same magazine, was a "glitzy and glamorous celebration" with guests including Thomas Friedman and India's "mining barons and real estate tycoons" held "at a five-star resort . . . allegedly owned by men in jail awaiting charges involving the 2G telecommunications scam."
28. Raman Kirpal,"How Goa's Illegal Ore Miners Are in League with CM Kamat," *First Post Politics*, September 5, 2011, http://www.firstpost.com/politics/how-goas-illegal-ore-miners-are-in-league-with-cm-kamat-76437.html.
29. Purnima S. Tripathi, "Battle of Bastar," *Frontline* 29, no. 8 (April/May 2012), http://www.frontline.in/navigation/?type=static&page=flonnet&rdurl=fl2908/stories/20120504290803200.htm.

30. "PIL on India Role in 'Genocide,'" *Telegraph India*, March 21, 2013, http://www.telegraphindia.com/1130321/jsp/nation/story_16698590.jsp#.Ud2nkuB1Pdk. Peter Cobus, "Indian Kashmir to ID Bodies from Unmarked Graves," *Voice of America*, September 26, 2011, http://www.voanews.com/content/indian-kashmir-to-id-bodies-from-unmarked-graves-130632003/168028.html.
31. Jaipur Sun, "Jaipur Lit Fest: Oprah Winfrey Charms Chaotic India," *Indian Express*, January 22, 2012, http://www.indianexpress.com/news/jaipur-lit-fest-oprah-winfrey-charms-chaotic-india/902640/.
32. Gerard Colby, *Thy Will Be Done: Conquest of the Amazon; Nelson Rockefeller and Evangelism in the Age of Oil* (New York: Harper Collins, 1996).
33. "Introduction: The Rockefellers," *American Experience*, Corporation for Public Broadcasting, http://www.pbs.org/wgbh/americanexperience/features/introduction/rockefellers-introduction/. "Because of the ruthless war he waged to crush his competitors, Rockefeller was to many Americans the embodiment of an unjust and cruel economic system. Yet he lived a quiet and virtuous life. 'I believe the power to make money is a gift of God,' Rockefeller once said. 'It is my duty to make money and even more money and to use the money I make for the good of my fellow men.'"
34. Pablo Neruda, "Standard Oil Company," in *Canto General*, trans. Jack Schmitt (Berkeley: University of California Press, 1991), 176.
35. For further analysis of the Gates Foundation's involvement in privatizing education, coupled with drastic reductions in government spending, see Jeff Bale and Sara Knopp, "Obama's Neoliberal Agenda for Public Education," in *Education and Capitalism: Struggles for Learning and Liberation* (Chicago: Haymarket Books, 2012).
36. Joan Roelofs, "The Third Sector as a Protective Layer for Capitalism," *Monthly Review* 47, no. 4 (September 1995): 16.
37. Joan Roelofs, *Foundations and Public Policy: The Mask of Pluralism*

(Albany, NY: SUNY Press, 2003).

38. Eric Toussaint, *Your Money or Your Life: The Tyranny of Global Finance* (Chicago: Haymarket Books, 2005).
39. Roelofs, "Third Sector."
40. Ibid.
41. Ibid.
42. Ibid.
43. Erika Kinetz, "Small Loans Add Up to Lethal Debts." *Hindu*, February 25, 2012 http://www.thehindu.com/news/national/small-loans-add-up-to-lethal-debts/article2932670.ece.
44. David Ransom, "Ford Country: Building an Elite in Indonesia," in *The Trojan Horse: A Radical Look at Foreign Aid*, ed. Steve Weissman with members of the Pacific Studies Center and the North American Congress on Latin America (Palo Alto, CA: Ramparts, 1975), 93–116.
45. Juan Gabriel Valdés, *Pinochet's Economists: The Chicago School of Economics in Chile* (New York: Cambridge University Press, 1995).
46. Rajander Singh Negi, "Magsaysay Award: Asian Nobel, Not So Noble," *Economic and Political Weekly* 43, no. 34 (2008): 14–16.
47. Narayan Lakshman,"World Bank Needs Anti-graft Policies," *Hindu*, September 1, 2011, http://www.thehindu.com/todays-paper/tp-international/world-bank-needs-antigraft-policies/article2416346.ece. Speaking to the *Hindu*, Navin Girishankar, one of the main authors of the World Bank's Independent Evaluation Group (IEG) study, said that "on the one hand there is a need to foster demand for good governance by helping improve the government responsiveness to pressures through greater transparency and more disclosure policies. . . . The Indian experience, including the Lokpal bills, might dovetail with this type of strategy."
48. Alejandra Viveros, "World Bank Announces Winners of Award for Outstanding Public Service," April 15, 2008, http://web.worldbank.org/

WBSITE/EXTERNAL/NEWS/0,,contentMDK:21732141 ~pagePK:34370~piPK:34424~theSitePK:4607,00.html.

49. See Roelofs, "Third Sector."
50. Press Trust of India, "Infosys to Bid for UID Projects, Sees No Conflict of Interest," *Indian Express*, June 27, 2009, http://www.indianexpress.com/news/infosys-to-bid-for-uid-projects-sees-no-conflict-of-interest/481849/.
51. Justin Gillis, "Bill Gates Calls for More Accountability on Food Programs," *New York Times*, February 23, 2012, http://green.blogs.nytimes.com/2012/02/23/bill-gates-calls-for-more-accountability-on-food-programs/.
52. Robert Arnove, ed., *Philanthropy and Cultural Imperialism: The Foundations at Home and Abroad* (Boston: G. K. Hall, 1980). In the essay "American Philanthropy and the Social Sciences," Donald Fisher outlines US foundations' role in shaping political thought through influence over university disciplines worldwide.
53. See http://foundationcenter.org/findfunders/topfunders/top100assets.html.
54. See Roelofs, *Foundations and Public Policy.*
55. Manning Marable, *Race, Reform, and Rebellion: The Second Reconstruction and Beyond in Black America, 1945–2006* (Jackson: University of Mississippi Press, 2007).
56. Devin Fergus, *Liberalism, Black Power, and the Making of American Politics, 1965–1980* (Athens: University of Georgia Press, 2009).
57. The Department of Defense links to the King Center's website and continues to play an active role in shaping how the United States celebrates King's legacy. See http://www.defense.gov/News/NewsArticle.aspx?ID=43313.
58. See Roelofs, "Third Sector."
59. P. Vaidyanathan Iyer, "Dalit Inc. Ready to Show Business Can Beat Caste," *Indian Express*, December 15, 2011, http://www.indianexpress

.com/news/dalit-inc.-ready-to-show-business-can-beat-caste/888062/.

60. See http://orfonline.org/cms/sites/orfonline/home.html. The ORF has also been directly involved in Modi's ascent: of Modi's participation in a conference hosted by Google, one ORF fellow said, "He is trying to project himself as a modern person who is keen on developmental issues and this summer offers him a platform to reach out to people of the younger generation—what we call aspirational India" (http://india.blogs.nytimes.com/2013/03/20/google-hosts-narendra-modi-at-tech-summit/).
61. See "Raytheon Aligns with Indian Companies to Pursue Emerging Opportunities," November 13, 2007, http://raytheon.mediaroom.com/index.php?s=43&item=870.
62. Engels and Marx, *Manifesto*.

CHAPTER 2: I'D RATHER NOT BE ANNA

1. "Anna Hazare Himself Involved in Corruption, Says Congress," *Economic Times*, August 14, 2011, http://articles.economictimes.indiatimes.com/2011-08-14/news/29886595_1_hind-swaraj-trust-anna-hazare-lokpal-bill. See also "Had Held Hazare Guilty of Corruption: PB Sawant," *IBNLive*, August 14, 2011.
2. Shortly after Hazare's release from prison, the *Telegraph* reported that Hazare was sustained with glucose and electrolyte powder during his second "fast unto death." Of the possible fraud, the physician who examined him, Abhijit Vaidya, offered an analysis: "I fear Hazare is being used as a tool to destabilise the government. . . . Corruption obviously needs to be fought but Hazare has never addressed other social issues such as economic inequality, extreme poverty and farmers' suicides that are equally hurting the country." "Secret of Fast? Hear It from a Pune Doctor," *Telegraph*, August 16, 2011, http://www.telegraphindia.com/1110817/jsp/nation/story_14386100.jsp. See

also "The Anna Hazare Scam," *Analytical Monthly Review*, April 15, 2011, http://mrzine.monthlyreview.org/2011/amr150411.html.

3. Manas Dasgupta, "Hazare Clarifies Remarks on Modi, But Activists Unrelenting," *Hindustan*, April 13, 2011, http://www.hindu.com/2011/04/13/stories/2011041364651600.htm.
4. "Hazare Failed to Recognise Workers' Contribution: RSS," *Hindu*, February 5, 2012, http://www.thehindu.com/news/national/hazare-failed-to-recognise-workers-contribution-rss/article2863182.ece.
5. Mukul Sharma, "The Making of Moral Authority: Anna Hazare and Watershed Management Programme in Ralegan Siddhi," *Economic and Political Weekly* 41, no. 20 (May 2006): 1981–88.
6. Lola Nayar, "Flowing the Way of Their Money," *Outlook India*, September 19, 2011, http://www.outlookindia.com/article.aspx?278264.

CHAPTER 3: DEAD MEN TALKING

1. Special correspondent, "Intellectuals Protest Deportation of US Broadcast-Writer," *Hindu*, September 29, 2011, http://www.thehindu.com/news/national/intellectuals-protest-deportation-of-us-broadcasterwriter/article2497779.ece.
2. Ibid. "When reached for comments, sources in the Home Ministry claimed that Mr. Barsamian had travelled to India without a 'valid visa.' However, sources at Delhi's IGI airport alleged that Mr. Barsamian had violated his visa norms during his visit in 2009–10 by indulging in professional work while holding a tourist visa. Thereafter, he was put on a watch list by the immigration authorities in order to prevent his entry on his next visit. The watch list was reviewed from time to time on the basis of inputs received from various quarters."
3. See "Kashmir: Time to Go," *Economist*, April 4, 2007, http://www.economist.com/node/8960457.

4. "US Professor Deported for 'Political Activism' in Valley," *Indian Express*, November 4, 2010, http://www.indianexpress.com/news/us-professor-deported-for—political-activism—in-valley/706855/. For a full report from the People's Tribunal on Human Rights and Justice, written by Angana P. Chatterji et al., see "Buried Evidence: Unknown, Unmarked, and Mass Graves in Indian-Administered Kashmir," November 2009, http://www.kashmirprocess.org/reports/graves/BuriedEvidenceKashmir.pdf.
5. See press note from the International People's Tribunal on Human Rights and Justice in Indian-Administered Kashmir: http://www.thekashmirwalla.com/2011/05/gautam-navlakha-denied-entry-deported-from-srinagar-airport-press-note-from-iptk/.
6. See 2013 report from the Committee to Protect Journalists: http://cpj.org/2013/07/for-journalist-in-chhattisgarh-justice-delayed-den.php.
7. See Shoma Chaudhury, "The Inconvenient Truth of Soni Sori," *Tehelka* 8, no. 41 (October 2011), http://archive.tehelka.com/story_main50.asp?filename=Ne151011coverstory.asp.
8. J. Venkatesan, "Salwa Judum Is Illegal, Says Supreme Court," *Hindu*, July 5, 2011, http://www.thehindu.com/news/national/salwa-judum-is-illegal-says-supreme-court/article2161246.ece.
9. See TehelkaTV video of the Chhattisgarh police official admitting to scripting Lingaram Kodopi's arrest after Kumar filed the habeas corpus petition: http://www.youtube.com/watch?v=qgtBZeLIuWs&list=PLz16ahsYEHrI1wNDNb56QpDATYZx0j8qw&index=1.
10. KumKum Desgupta, "Those Discordant Notes," *Hindustan Times*, September 20, 2011, http://www.hindustantimes.com/editorial-views-on/ColumnsOthers/Those-discordant-notes/Article1-748175.aspx.
11. Mohua Chatterjee and Vishwa Mohan, "Azad Killing a Big Blow to Maoists," *Economic Times*, July 3, 2010, http://articles.economictimes.indiatimes.com/2010-07-03/news/27581751_1_cherukuri

-rajkumar-maoists-dandakaranya.
12. Aman Sethi, "Maoists Announce Azad's Successor," *Hindu*, July 21, 2010, http://www.thehindu.com/todays-paper/tp-national/maoists-announce-azads-successor/article525724.ece.
13. Supriya Sharma, "Security Forces Running Riot in Dantewada?" *Times of India*, March 23, 2011, http://articles.timesofindia.indiatimes.com/2011-03-23/india/29177593_1_dantewada-villages-local-police.
14. See http://www.youtube.com/watch?v=LR4BdBWoPC0.
15. "Civil Rights Activist Binayak Sen Gets Bail," *Times of India*, May 25, 2009, http://articles.timesofindia.indiatimes.com/2009-05-25/india/28202410_1_plea-binayak-sen-chhattisgarh-high-court.
16. Shoma Chaudhury, "The Doctor, the State, and a Sinister Case," *Tehelka* 5, no. 7 (February 2008), http://archive.tehelka.com/story_main37.asp?filename=Ne230208The_Doctor.asp.
17. "Vanvasi Chetana Ashram Faces State Repression," Association for India's Development, http://aidindia.org/main/content/view/908/343/.
18. Tusha Mittal, "Where Is Our Savior?" *Tehelka* 49, no. 7 (December 2010). See also Amnesty International human rights abuses report: http://www.amnesty.org/en/library/asset/ASA20/023/2009/en/b017737b-8810-4b37-a8fa-6e9a7fbfa534/asa200232009en.pdf.
19. See public statement from Amnesty International, November 10, 2010: http://www.amnesty.org/en/library/asset/ASA20/031/2010/en/d7b90262-946e-4fb2-9b1e-4974cc01bc16/asa200312010en.html.

CHAPTER 4: KASHMIR'S FRUITS OF DISCORD

1. Joe Klein, "The Full Obama Interview," *Time*, October 23, 2008. http://swampland.time.com/2008/10/23/the_full_obama_interview/.
2. Sheryl Gay Stolberg and Jim Yardley, "Countering China, Obama

Backs India for U.N. Council," *New York Times*, November 8, 2010, http://www.nytimes.com/2010/11/09/world/asia/09prexy.html?page wanted=1&hp.

3. Yusuf Jameel and Lydia Polgreen, "Indian Agency Insists 2 Kashmiri Women Drowned," *New York Times*, December 14, 2009, http://www.nytimes.com/2009/12/15/world/asia/15kashmir.html?fta=y. Human Rights Watch Asia authored a report on the high incidence of rape by Indian security personnel. See "Rape in Kashmir: A Crime of War," Asia Watch (division of Human Rights Watch) and Physicians for Human Rights, vol. 5, no. 9 (2009), http://www.hrw.org/sites/default/files/reports/INDIA935.PDF.
4. Special correspondent, "Bajrang Dal's Warning to Arundhati Roy," *Hindu*, October 28, 2010, http://www.thehindu.com/news/national/bajrang-dals-warning-to-arundhati-roy/article853157.ece.

CHAPTER 5: A PERFECT DAY FOR DEMOCRACY

1. Sandeep Joshi and Ashok Kumar, "Afzal Guru Hanged in Secrecy, Buried in Tihar Jail," *Hindu*, February 9, 2013, http://www.thehindu.com/news/national/afzal-guru-hanged-in-secrecy-buried-in-tihar-jail/article4396289.ece. Even the lawyers who argued for his death sentence decried the secret hanging as a "human rights violation." See Manoj Mitta, "Afzal Guru's Secret Hanging a Human Rights Violation: Prosecutor," *Times of India*, February 13, 2013, http://articles.timesofindia.indiatimes.com/2013-02-13/india/37078504_1_afzal-guru-mercy-petition-parliament-attack.
2. See Joshi and Kumar, "Afzal Guru Hanged in Secrecy."
3. Sumegha Gulati, "SAR Geelani, Iftikhar among Those Placed under Detention," *Indian Express*, February 10, 2013, http://www.indianexpress.com/news/sar-geelani-iftikhar-among-those-placed-under-detention/1072061/. During the trial, Geelani was presented as

the mastermind of the 2001 attack, though he was eventually acquitted.

4. Mohammad Ali, "Muslim Groups See Political Motives," *Hindu*, February 11, 2013, http://www.thehindu.com/news/national/muslim-groups-see-political-motives/article4401021.ece.

CHAPTER 6: CONSEQUENCES OF HANGING AFZAL GURU

1. Ahmed Ali Fayyaz, "Two Days after Hanging, Letter Reaches Azfal's Wife," *Hindu*, February 11, 2013, http://www.thehindu.com/news/national/otherstates/two-days-after-hanging-letter-reaches-afzals-wife/article4403636.ece. Fayyaz notes, "Seals and signatures on the communication make it clear that the letter was written on February 6, or three days after the mercy petition was rejected, and dispatched only a day before the execution," making it clear that the late notice was deliberate.
2. News desk, "Kashmir's One Month since Afzal Guru's Hanging: 350 Civilians, 150 Cops Injured, 4 Dead," *Kashmir Walla*, March 10, 2013, http://www.thekashmirwalla.com/2013/03/kashmir-350-civilians-150-cops-injured-4-dead/.
3. See "Afzal Guru Papers" online: "Full Text: Supreme Court Judgement on Parliament Attack Convict Afzal Guru." IBNlive.in.com, February, 9, 2013, http://ibnlive.in.com/news/full-text-supreme-court-judgement-on-parliament-attack-convict-afzal-guru/371782-3.html. See also Arundhati Roy, ed., *A Reader: The Strange Case of the Attack on the Indian Parliament* (New Delhi: Penguin Books India, 2006), and Nirmalangshu Mukherji, *December 13: Terror over Democracy* (New Delhi: Promilla, 2005).
4. "Short of Participating in the Actual Attack, He Did Everything . . . ," *Indian Express*, February 10, 2013, http://www.indianexpress.com/news/-short-of-participating-in-the-actual-attack-he-did-everything...-/1072027/.

5. “Afzal Guru Papers”: “There is no evidence that [Afzal] is a member of a terrorist gang or a terrorist organization, once the confessional statement is excluded. Incidentally, we may mention that even going by confessional statement, it is doubtful whether the membership of a terrorist gang or organization is established.”
6. Praveen Swami, “Terrorism in Jammu and Kashmir in Theory and Practice,” *India Review* 2 (July 2003). See also Muhammad Amir Rana, *A to Z of Jehadi Organizations in Pakistan* (Lahore, Pakistan: Mashal Books, 2004).
7. See Yug Mohit Chaudhry, “Why Balwant Singh Rajoana Shouldn’t Be Hanged,” *Hindu*, March 29, 2012, http://www.thehindu.com/opinion/op-ed/article3255057.ece.
8. For new evidence on just how deliberate the hanging was, see “Government Behind Parliament Attack, 26/11: Ishrat Probe Officer,” *Times of India*, July 14, 2013, http://timesofindia.indiatimes.com/india/Govt-behind-Parliament-attack-26/11-Ishrat-probe-officer/articleshow/21062116.cms.
9. Bashaarat Masood, “The Grand (Standing) Mufti of Kasmir,” *Indian Express*, February 7, 2013, http://m.indianexpress.com/news/the-grand-(standing)-mufti-of-kashmir/1070526/. See also http://m.indianexpress.com/news/j-k-lawyer-to-challenge-grand-mufti-s-status/1070521/ and http://bigstory.ap.org/article/kashmir-girl-band-breaks-after-threats.
10. Aijaz Hussain, “Kashmir Police Publish Nuclear War Survival Tips,” Associated Press, January 22, 2013, http://bigstory.ap.org/article/india-warns-kashmiris-possible-nuclear-attack.

CHAPTER 7: SPEECH TO THE PEOPLE’S UNIVERSITY

1. Andrea Shalai-Esa, “Saudi Deals Boosted US Arms Sales to Record 66.3 Billion in 2011,” Reuters UK, August 27, 2012,

http://uk.reuters.com/article/2012/08/27/uk-usa-arms-sales-idUKBRE87Q0UT20120827.

2. Stephen P. Cohen and Sunil Dasgupta, "Arms Sales for India," *Foreign Affairs*, March/April 2011, http://www.foreignaffairs.com/articles/67462/sunil-dasgupta-and-stephen-p-cohen/arms-sales-for-india.
3. "Mukesh Ambani Tops for the Third Year as India's Richest," *Forbes Asia*, news release, September 30, 2010. The article notes, "The combined net worth of India's 100 richest people is $300 billion, up from $276 billion last year. This year, there are 69 billionaires on the India Rich List, 17 more than last year." India's 2009 GDP was $1.2 trillion.
4. P. Sainath, "Farm Suicides Rise in Maharashtra, State Still Leads the List," *Hindu*, July 3, 2012, www.thehindu.com/opinion/columns/sainath/article3595351.ece.

INDEX

ABOUT HAYMARKET BOOKS

Haymarket Books is a nonprofit, progressive book distributor and publisher, a project of the Center for Economic Research and Social Change. We believe that activists need to take ideas, history, and politics into the many struggles for social justice today. Learning the lessons of past victories, as well as defeats, can arm a new generation of fighters for a better world. As Karl Marx said, "The philosophers have merely interpreted the world; the point, however, is to change it."

We take inspiration and courage from our namesakes, the Haymarket Martyrs, who gave their lives fighting for a better world. Their 1886 struggle for the eight-hour day reminds workers around the world that ordinary people can organize and struggle for their own liberation.

For more information and to shop our complete catalog of titles, visit us online at www.haymarketbooks.org.

ALSO FROM HAYMARKET BOOKS

Field Notes on Democracy: Listening to Grasshoppers
Arundhati Roy

Until My Freedom Has Come: The New Intifada in Kashmir
Edited by Sanjay Kak

The Battle for Justice in Palestine
Ali Abunimah

ABOUT THE AUTHOR

© SANJAY KAK

Arundhati Roy was born in 1959 in Shillong, India. She studied architecture in New Delhi, where she now lives. She has worked as a film designer and screenplay writer in India. Roy is the author of the novel *The God of Small Things*, for which she received the 1997 Booker Prize. The novel has been translated into dozens of languages worldwide. She has written several nonfiction books, including *The Cost of Living*, *Power Politics*, *War Talk*, *An Ordinary Person's Guide to Empire*, and *Public Power in the Age of Empire*. Roy was featured in the BBC television documentary *Dam/age*, which is about the struggle against big dams in India. A collection of interviews with Arundhati Roy by David Barsamian was published as *The Checkbook and the Cruise Missile*. She is a contributor to the Verso anthology *Kashmir: The Case for Freedom*. Her newest books are *Field Notes on Democracy: Listening to Grasshoppers*, published by Haymarket Books, and *Walking with the Comrades*, published by Penguin. Roy is the recipient of the 2002 Lannan Foundation Cultural Freedom Prize.